YANKEES MADE SIMPLER

YANKEES
MADE SIMPLER

By Michael Hicks

Texas
Monthly®
Press

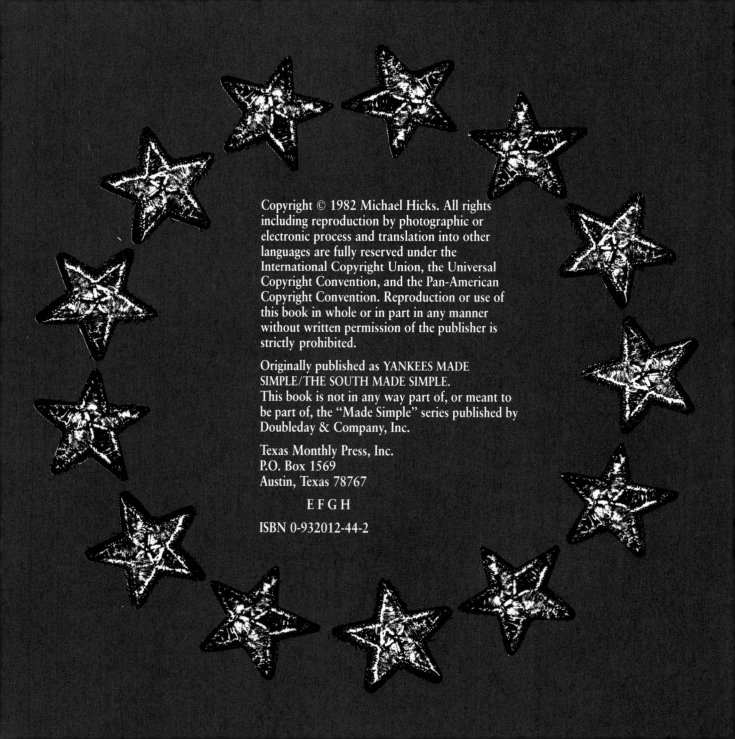

Originally published as YANKEES MADE
SIMPLE/THE SOUTH MADE SIMPLE.
This book is not in any way part of, or meant to
be part of, the "Made Simple" series published by
Doubleday & Company, Inc.

Texas Monthly Press, Inc.
P.O. Box 1569
Austin, Texas 78767

E F G H

ISBN 0-932012-44-2

Book Design: Hixo, Inc.

Artwork by Tom Ballenger, Laura Eisenhour,
Mike Hicks, Richard Krall, Claire Maeder,
Larry Don McEntire, Fran Pelzman, Tom Poth,
Harrison Saunders, Bob Scott, David Bob Shapiro,
Janet Tindel, and K.L. (the Mystery Woman).

Cover Photo: Stence & Stence.

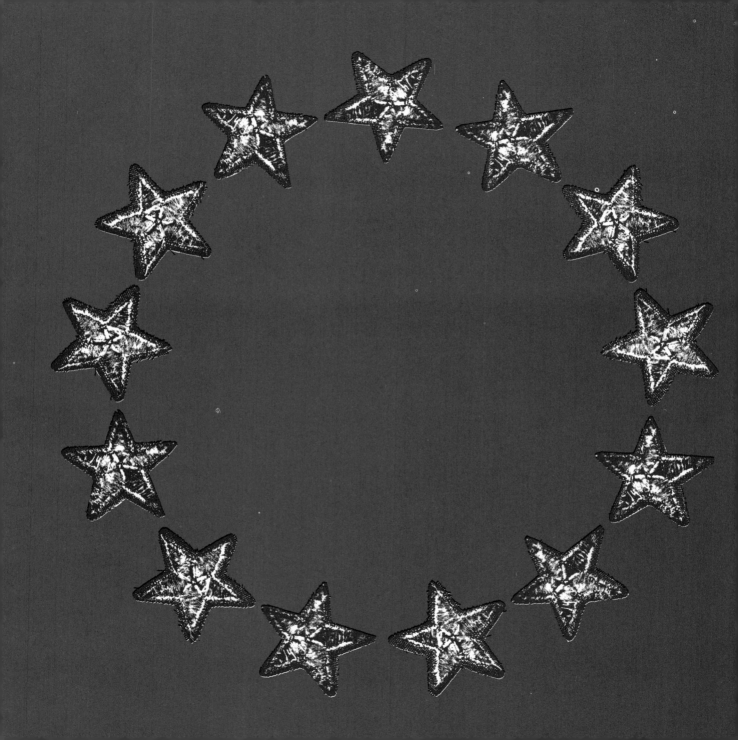

THE INSIDER THEORY

Understanding the Yankee mentality can be extremely difficult for the average Southerner. This is due, in no small part, to the fact that most Southerners presume that everyone either has or desires a large amount of space and a sense of the outdoors. However, Yankees are an interior, furtive group. You have but to look at their various habitats to get an idea. For instance, most have basements (small concrete rooms) under their houses. Entire families often congregate in these subterranean rooms—for pleasure. In the larger cities Yankees build up and down, stacking room upon room. The upper floors of these skyscrapers are dearly valued because the residents can go further down from them. They put their plants inside, in greenhouses. They brought you bowling alleys. And what about subways? Everyone's underground in the North. Even most of the train stations are inside and down. Look at Grand Central. Even in automobiles, they go for tunnels. In New England, they even cover the bridges. And who do you think brought you the station wagon? Just a bunch of Yankees who didn't want to ride outside in the back of a pickup, that's who.

And vegetables: all root plants! Carrots, turnips, potatoes . . . You get the idea. Yankees have "inside jokes," and can often be heard giving another fellow "inside information" or an "inside tip" on the stock market. And something that's really popular is "in this season" in the North, whereas the South has always referred to this condition with words like "far out" or "hot."

When transplanted to the South, it takes a displaced Yankee several weeks to adjust to seeing the horizon without becoming dizzy, to be exposed to full sunlight without hissing. Maybe it's best to think of your new Yankee neighbors as reformed vampires visiting a church for the first time.

Yankees can be divided into several basic types. Most Yankees can be defined as "persons not living in the South," but as with all rules, there are several exceptions. For instance, there are many people who, through an unfortunate accident of birth, should have been Southerners but have grown up thinking that they were Yankees simply because they had parents who were. Most of these didn't fare too well in the society in which they were reared, and they left for the South the moment the opportunity presented itself. The remaining few must only be pitied for their lack of resolve. Fortunately, true unrepentant Yankees can be typed, and thus easily identified.

New Yorkers. This is a type not limited to the state of New York. They talk funny, live in apartments they call "houses," and believe they have a true grip on how life should be lived. They honestly believe that hardship builds character, but almost always try to insulate themselves from any real character building. Inventors of deficit spending, three-piece underwear, subways, and penny loafers, they are clearly not to be underestimated.

New Englanders. These folks seldom venture out of the Northeast. Their better traits include crabbiness, clannishness, irascibility, and a distrust of anything modern. Most have the smell of goosedown and twenty-year-old periodicals about them, and they will often be seen wearing cherished garments that they value in direct proportion to the threadbare spots on the sleeves. These are the people who brought you the baked bean, the kidney bean, and L. L. Bean. They fancy themselves to be educated, but you have to ask yourself: Why are they still living in the cold zone?

TYPES

Motorheads. This group includes any-one from Michigan and the surrounding area, a region currently being transferred, intact, to Houston. Worker bees in search of a warm hive, they are recognizable by their extreme pallors, their lust for beer and pizza, and an unhealthy attachment to labor unions.

Californians. Transients in search of another trend to follow, notable for skin that's too tan and diets that don't include meat. Almost everything that Southerners value, they find disgusting. If you want to meet a Californian, run a small ad in your newspaper offering ferns and redwood planks for sale.

Snowbirds. These folks come from places where it's cold. Very, very cold. Each January, they head south, sporting their telltale plumage of mittens and sunglasses.

In a great number of professions, the Southerner will confront the necessity of traveling north, often to New York City. This can be a pleasant experience or an incredibly bad one. Naturally, the powers of evil only prey on the innocent and uninformed, but because there are so many evil powers lurking in NYC, one should take some precautions that might seem extreme in other towns. Here are a few basics that will keep you from appearing like fresh bait to the locals:

Don't eat any barbeque, anywhere. You will be disappointed at best, and very, very ill at worst.

Don't carry cameras with you. On top of making you look like a geek, your Kodak will proclaim to all the world that you are a visitor waiting to be mugged.

Never tell a cabbie the best way to get to where you're going. Even if you know the best way, the fare will surely be higher because the driver's heart will not be in it.

Never take a subway anywhere. If man had been meant to travel underground, he would have been given larger eyes. Additionally, there's no quicker way to find yourself miles away from Manhattan in a neighborhood where everyone wants your watch. Many Southerners have disappeared this way.

Constantly looking up at the buildings and gawking around is the equivalent to wearing a "HURT ME" sign.

Never go into Union Square at night seeking change for a hundred.

Never go into Union Square at night.

Never go into Union Square.

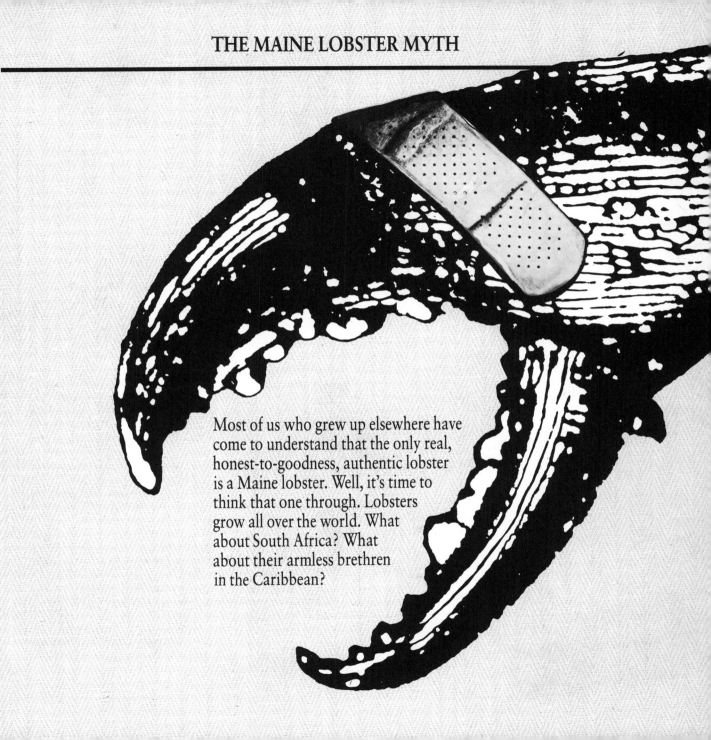

Most of us who grew up elsewhere have come to understand that the only real, honest-to-goodness, authentic lobster is a Maine lobster. Well, it's time to think that one through. Lobsters grow all over the world. What about South Africa? What about their armless brethren in the Caribbean?

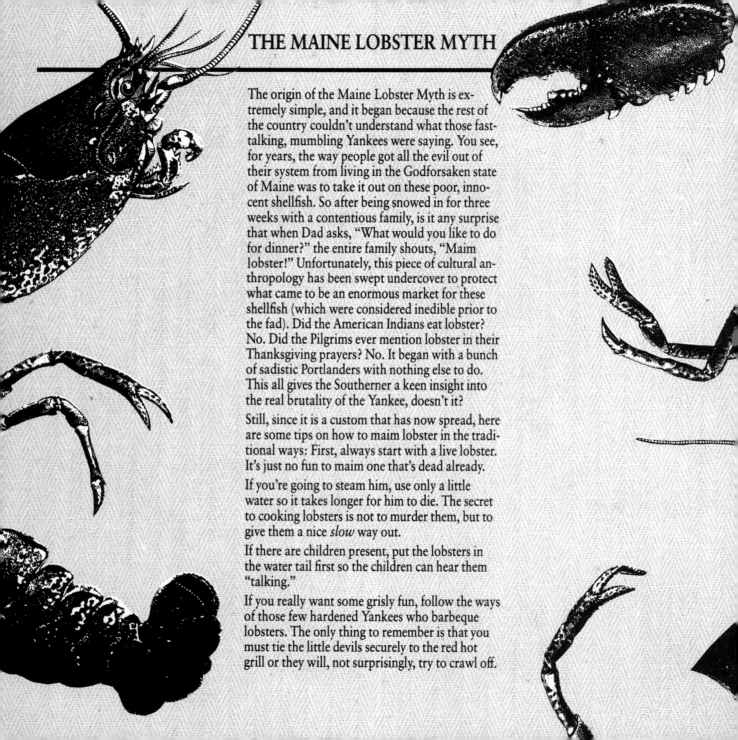

THE MAINE LOBSTER MYTH

The origin of the Maine Lobster Myth is extremely simple, and it began because the rest of the country couldn't understand what those fast-talking, mumbling Yankees were saying. You see, for years, the way people got all the evil out of their system from living in the Godforsaken state of Maine was to take it out on these poor, innocent shellfish. So after being snowed in for three weeks with a contentious family, is it any surprise that when Dad asks, "What would you like to do for dinner?" the entire family shouts, "Maim lobster!" Unfortunately, this piece of cultural anthropology has been swept undercover to protect what came to be an enormous market for these shellfish (which were considered inedible prior to the fad). Did the American Indians eat lobster? No. Did the Pilgrims ever mention lobster in their Thanksgiving prayers? No. It began with a bunch of sadistic Portlanders with nothing else to do. This all gives the Southerner a keen insight into the real brutality of the Yankee, doesn't it?

Still, since it is a custom that has now spread, here are some tips on how to maim lobster in the traditional ways: First, always start with a live lobster. It's just no fun to maim one that's dead already.

If you're going to steam him, use only a little water so it takes longer for him to die. The secret to cooking lobsters is not to murder them, but to give them a nice *slow* way out.

If there are children present, put the lobsters in the water tail first so the children can hear them "talking."

If you really want some grisly fun, follow the ways of those few hardened Yankees who barbeque lobsters. The only thing to remember is that you must tie the little devils securely to the red hot grill or they will, not surprisingly, try to crawl off.

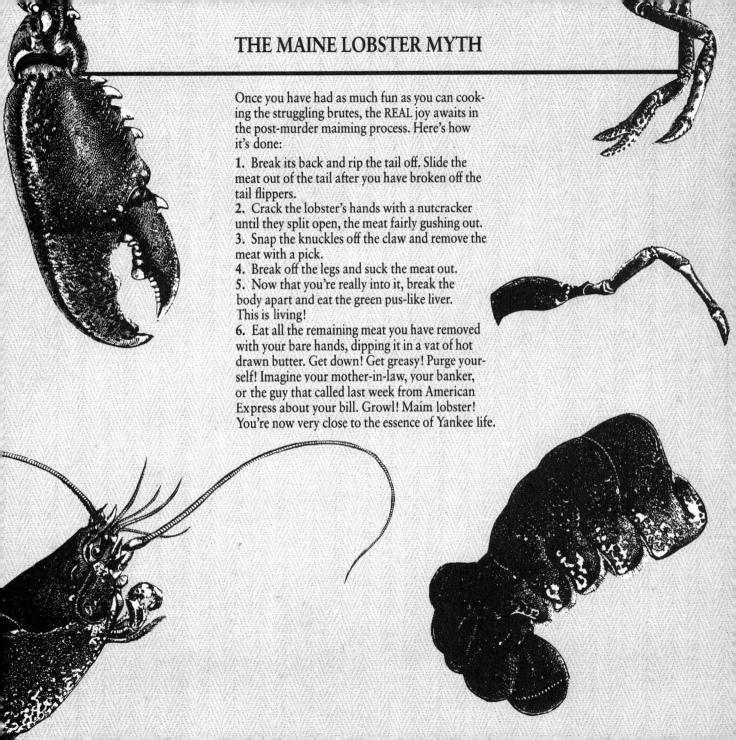

THE MAINE LOBSTER MYTH

Once you have had as much fun as you can cooking the struggling brutes, the REAL joy awaits in the post-murder maiming process. Here's how it's done:

1. Break its back and rip the tail off. Slide the meat out of the tail after you have broken off the tail flippers.

2. Crack the lobster's hands with a nutcracker until they split open, the meat fairly gushing out.

3. Snap the knuckles off the claw and remove the meat with a pick.

4. Break off the legs and suck the meat out.

5. Now that you're really into it, break the body apart and eat the green pus-like liver. This is living!

6. Eat all the remaining meat you have removed with your bare hands, dipping it in a vat of hot drawn butter. Get down! Get greasy! Purge yourself! Imagine your mother-in-law, your banker, or the guy that called last week from American Express about your bill. Growl! Maim lobster! You're now very close to the essence of Yankee life.

Often, one will notice that there is a certain look to most Yankees. If you are ever going to mix with them, then it might be a good idea to know how to bring off a decent imitation so that you don't stand out. When in the South, many Yankees abandon their quaint dress habits due to the well-known Southern distaste for earmuffs.

DRESSING YANKEE

Umbrella. A standard. No one goes anywhere without an umbrella lurking somewhere close. These also double as weapons in the city, and they are absolutely essential in New York. Many locals file the points to razor sharpness.

Arm-Tied Sweaters. This is true hubba-hubba, East Coast style. Keeps one perpetually prepared for a sudden freak blizzard.

Duck Patterns. Another strange predilection. Nothing is as irresistible to the true Northerner. Ties are a favorite, but virtually anything—shirts, hats, underwear, toilet paper—is believed enhanced if there are a few mallards on it.

Goosedown. Almost anything is believed to be better if it has been stuffed with goosedown. This includes underwear, socks, belts, and ties.

Two Shirts. Presumably, if wearing one expensive shirt is good, then wearing two is even better. Tough on laundry bills.

Plaid Pants. Among some Yankees there is a wild, primeval desire to own plaid pants. Invaluable for blending in at a punk furniture auction.

Designer Jeans. These are a must. No longer can you rely on one pair, either, since "in" designers change quite rapidly. This is fortunate, because the jeans rarely outlast the popularity of their maker, anyway.

CABS

In many Northern cities, cabs are the main means of getting about. People pride themselves on their ability to find a cab in remote areas when it is raining and often—just to test their mettle—go to dark, dangerous sections of the city when they think a storm is coming.

A Yankee without cab service is like a man with no legs. Many don't understand the concept of no cabs and don't recognize that the only people who take cabs in the South are either too elderly to drive or have no friends to take them to the airport. Newcomers to the South will often call the cab service and take a few hours' ride just because they miss it so much. In fact, there's nothing quite so pitiful as watching a grown Yankee try to find a cab in the South. It's clear to everyone that this person is from somewhere far, far away. There are few easier ways to be run over than by stepping off the curb in, say, Charlotte, North Carolina, and sticking a hand or an old umbrella in the air.

When you can find them, you'll learn that Southern cab drivers usually are more personable than their Northern counterparts. Most Northern cabbies are mutes and often only grunt to their

customers. The only time a Northern cabbie can be forced to speak is if he has been short-fared or if some other motorist gets in his way. In the South, cabbies drive at a leisurely pace. In the North, the only way to win a cabbie's heart is to ask one to get you a ridiculous distance in an impossible time. Southerners like to drive themselves if they are going to be in a race, but Yankees prefer to have a driver while racing so that they can experience the adrenalin rush from the comfort of the worn, stained, lumpy back seat of a Checker. The world's record for the run from 59th Street and Fifth Avenue to La Guardia Airport now stands at a little under eight minutes and is held by Alfonse Ritalle of Brooklyn, a man much admired for his unique tunnel driving style. The passenger suffered a massive stroke during Ritalle's power slide onto the Triborough Bridge and was unable to pay the fare or catch the plane, so the record run was marred. While cab racing continues as one of the most popular of Northern sports, it regrettably remains merely a service in the South.

MANNERS

One thing most Southerners will notice immediately about the North is the basic absence of the small pleasantries that we call manners. The closer to a city, the more noticeable the absence. So as not to appear a hopeless wimp, one should be aware of those things that are not practiced in the North. For instance, something as inconsequential as opening the door for a woman can keep you tied up all day in a place like Chicago.

Yankee Manners.	Southern Manners.
	Don't spit on the sidewalk.
	Tip your hat to a woman.
	Open a car door for a woman.
	Allow a woman to enter a room first.
	Pay for a lady's drinks.
	Pay for a lady's meal.
	Walk to the outside of a sidewalk when with a woman.
	Stand when a woman enters a room.
	Offer your wrap to a cold woman.
	Offer your umbrella to a wet woman.
	Don't smoke in the presence of a woman without asking permission.
	Don't swear in the presence of a woman.
	Greet strangers with a pleasant " hello."
	Never strike an opponent while he's down.
	Always say "sir" or "ma'am" to anyone older than you.
	Always say "please" and "thank you."
	Don't eat with your hands (except BBQ and fried chicken).
	Keep your elbows off the table.
	Don't grab.

The earliest pilgrims to this great country of ours had a lot to do just to stay alive. There were so many things out to get them, in fact, that food was the last thing on their minds. This proved to be an unfortunate precedent for the generations to come. Not that the Yankees weren't curious. They tried eating a lot of unusual things just to stay alive. Their big mistake was that when they found anything, absolutely anything, that would support life, it became a part of their cuisine. If the food wasn't vile enough on its own to ease the conscience of our puritanical forefathers, it would be made so by the local method of preparation. No wonder the Indians quit going to those Thanksgiving dinners.

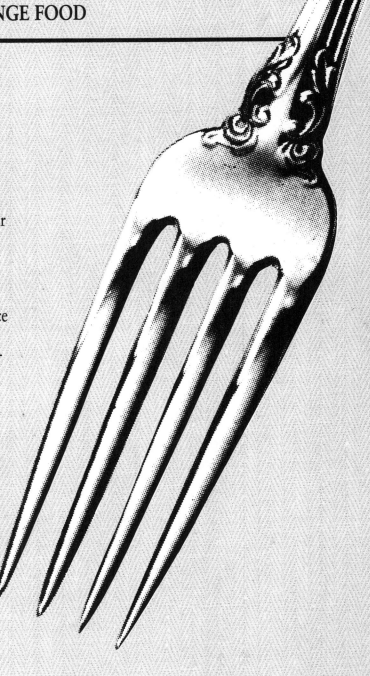

STRANGE FOOD

Submarine Sandwiches. Long renowned as gourmets, the men of this country's nuclear navy have this sandwich as their lasting legacy to the culinary arts of the nation. The submarine sandwich, which was developed by the Department of the Navy during World War II, stores well and will withstand a damp environment for months. Knowing its origins, it is easier to understand why good ones always give the diner that unmistakable sinking feeling.

Baby Back Ribs. This Yankee concession to BBQ is a cruel hoax. Most people assume that the ribs come from some part of a young calf, when in fact the ribs are smuggled out of foundling hospitals. This is an outrage, an inhumane offense to everything on which this great country was founded, and a reasonably good appetizer.

New England Boiled Dinner. The mother of all New England food. Simple to make, tough to eat. What you do is take a roast, or any other piece of meat that you might find, put it in a pot with potatoes, carrots, cabbage, and any other vegetables you have, add water (and salt if you are the continental type), and start the dish boiling. After a few days or so, take it off and eat it. You can tell it's done when the colors of its components, from the beef to the carrots, represent the entire spectrum of the color gray.

Tastie Kakes. The forerunner of the Twinkie. A sweet filled pastry in tubular form that has a large following in the Philadelphia area. Those who eat Tastie Kakes are generally shaped like Tastie Kakes.

Crab or Fish Cakes. Originally served only in bars as an appetizer; this should tell you something. The idea was that a host of lesser known parts of the crab or fish could be put into a batter and deep fried into anonymity, so those who indulged never actually had to encounter the grisly sight of crab nostrils in their meal. As might have been expected, Yankees developed a taste for fish cakes and started serving them in their homes. Later, some bright boys on Madison Avenue decided a financially strapped public might fall for fish sticks.

Cheese Steak. A poor substitute for a hamburger. An even poorer substitute for a chicken-fried steak. An extremely good substitute for a can of ribs.

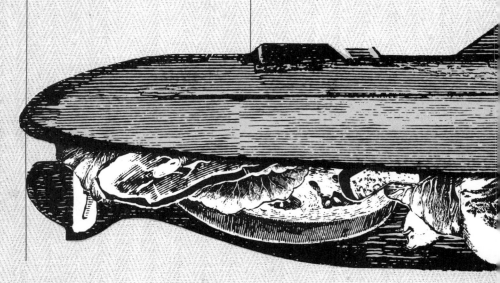

STRANGE FOOD

Soft Pretzels. Many Southerners think that pretzels only come in the crunchy version. Not so. In fact, they are all soft in the beginning, but if no one buys them and they dry up, the Yankees ship them South. The galling truth is that Southerners have been eating leftover pretzels for years, to the constant amusement of the Yanks. Now that a good number of Yankees are living in the South, this is no longer tolerated and you can actually buy fresh pretzels in most major cities in the South. About time!

Scrapple. One of several foods that Yankees feed to their in-laws. Scrapple is various inside parts of the pig that are ground up and then either tied link-style into intestine casings or made into patties and fried. Sounds great, huh? Sausage for the depraved. If you serve scrapple daily, most members of the household will be driven to other quarters; thus has it been found that in more than ninety percent of the homes that have a mother-in-law as a permanent resident, scrapple is missing from the diet. This Missing Link strategy has proven remarkably effective in many parts of the North, and any Southerner who is served scrapple in a Yankee's home can rest assured he has overstayed his welcome.

Clam Chowder. Sort of the chili of the North. Every area on the East Coast has its own version of basic clam soup with something added. As with all broad-appeal items, there are factions. Most notable among the clam chowder addicts are the Tomato vs. No Tomato factions. Manhattan chowder has tomatoes and no cream, Rhode Island Red has tomatoes and cream, New England has cream but no tomatoes, and Detroit clam chowder has tomatoes, cream, and STP.

Saltwater Taffy. A basic candy in the North, as well as a source of amusement. It originated in Atlantic City when a flood spilled portions of the New Jersey ocean (and its sand, muck, and fauna) into a batch of basically normal taffy. Locals still prefer the seafood version and are often seen dragging long sheets of the candy along the beach behind them for seasoning.

STREET SPORTS

In the North, space is at a premium; consequently, people have invented a number of sports that can only be played on the street. Even though the championship players will receive only local press, it's really the sport that matters. Here are a few you might see in the cities:

Stickball. The only essentials are a broom and a squishy ball called a "spaldeen." The game is played like baseball, but is infinitely more interesting due to the differences in the playing field. Bases usually go something like this: First is the fireplug, second is the red Buick, and third is Joey's little brother. Most Northern city children grow up playing stickball, and the accomplished start playing on turnpikes in their teens.

Stoopball. A two-man combination of handball and baseball. Facing the wall, one player throws the ball against the steps of a tenement. The opponent seeks to catch it before it bounces. One bounce before it is caught is a single, two bounces is a double, three is a triple, over the fielder's head is a homer. The entire opposing team can be wiped out by a bus if the fly ball is deep enough.

Car Stripping. Here's a popular one. Cars are classified by difficulty, and a four-man team races against the clock. The record for Porsches is around eighteen minutes down to the bare frame, with extra points given for air-conditioned models.

ACTUAL
SCALE
DRAWING

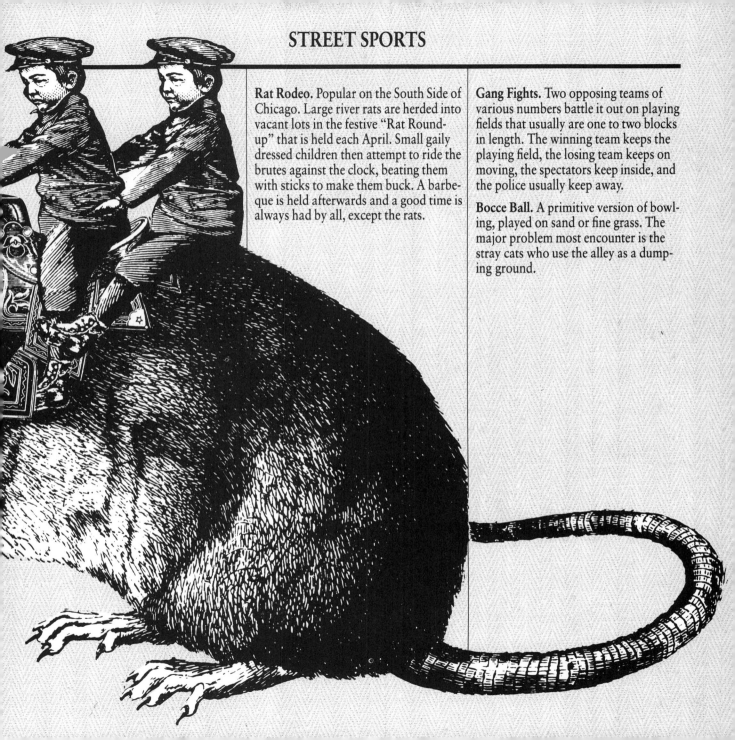

STREET SPORTS

Rat Rodeo. Popular on the South Side of Chicago. Large river rats are herded into vacant lots in the festive "Rat Round-up" that is held each April. Small gaily dressed children then attempt to ride the brutes against the clock, beating them with sticks to make them buck. A barbeque is held afterwards and a good time is always had by all, except the rats.

Gang Fights. Two opposing teams of various numbers battle it out on playing fields that usually are one to two blocks in length. The winning team keeps the playing field, the losing team keeps on moving, the spectators keep inside, and the police usually keep away.

Bocce Ball. A primitive version of bowling, played on sand or fine grass. The major problem most encounter is the stray cats who use the alley as a dumping ground.

Shiver in their presence.

Ask to borrow an umbrella.

Complain of heat rashes from your recent trip to Atlanta.

Ask how to make a daiquiri.

Refuse to wear your Honda T-shirt in Detroit.

Offer to buy their house.

NORTHERN BELLES

A creation of the medical profession, the Northern belle, also known as the Jewish American Princess, is born with shopping in her blood and is taught to figure discounts at an early age. These girls are the retailer's best friends, particularly when armed with a trust fund. Most are born with silver spoons in their mouths, which proves useful throughout life: Open your mouth, and Daddy will fork over some more silver. The most stressful experience in one of these creature's lives occurs during the transition from Doctor Father to Doctor Husband, and many credit ratings have been stretched to their limits during these sensitive years.

Several things are required for the potential suitor. In addition to a medical degree, he also must possess a diamond ring the size of a golf ball, a platinum American Express card, and a very strong back. This last is required if you plan to travel with a Jewish American Princess, because of a genetic trait that causes her skin to fester if exposed to the same piece of clothing more than once; thus, ten bags of clothing, as well as some forty to sixty pounds of cosmetics, are about standard for the average weekend trip.

Northern Belle Friends: Loehmann's, American Express, diet soft drinks, Bonwit Teller, Tiffany, Mona's Nails, hair spray, Gloria Vanderbilt, Gucci, electrolysis, Godiva chocolates, and psychiatrists.

Northern Belle Enemies: Bankruptcy referees, designer knock-offs, sugar, cellulite, sunburn, overdrafts, Godiva chocolates, and, worst of all, allergies, especially to gold and other precious metals.

LIBERALS

A particularly strange form of Yankee that the Southerner will likely confront in the North is the Affluent Liberal. These folks are different from anything you have ever dealt with in the South and should be regarded with caution at all times. While many people tend to pity the Liberal, you should never assume that they are simply defective Dixiecrats. They are an entirely different and misguided species.

Here are eight easy ways to identify them:

1. They believe that political parties should differ from one another on issues.

2. They never use the short form to report their taxes, but always feel guilty about it.

3. They read books to excess.

4. They have the unfulfilled desire to be the victims of something.

5. They attend theatres where dinner is not served.

6. They attend rock concerts in order to save whales.

7. They have their maids address them by first name.

8. They tip too much.

LIBERALS

YANKEE SHOES

Topsiders. Designed for the tops of what? Yachts? Canoes? Less than one percent of their wearers have ever seen the open sea, but not owning a pair or two will label you as a free-thinker in many circles.

Slip-On Tennis Shoes. The ultimate in geek attire. A more useless shoe would be hard to imagine, but the inventors of the slip-on are probably working on something like slip-on mountain climbing boots at this very minute.

Penny Loafers. A standard fixture, but one that has suffered from inflation. Nowadays, the truly chic are loading them with all those leftover Susan B. Anthony dollars. A grim sign for economists everywhere.

Black Pointers. The favorites of anyone who knows and follows ethnic music. These are dancing shoes, the points telegraphing your general direction to your dancing partner. Also good for a quick but effective kick to the ankles of anyone crowding you.

YANKEE SHOES

Hightop Basketball Shoes. Designed in the North for athletes plagued with frostbite of the ankles.

House Slippers. Worn in the South by cripples and the elderly, but a necessity if you're thin blooded and living in the North. Truly a difficult shoe to wear respectably. Most people look hopelessly sissy in even the most macho of house slippers.

Galoshes. The most cumbersome of all footwear, including snowshoes. Elementary schools give lessons on how to put on galoshes, but they still defy all but the extremely coordinated. Grown men have been known to scream trying to put a pair on in a hurry. For some reason, one always goes on easier than the other.

Duck Shoes. Many people think that these shoes were named because of the tops, which resemble duckfeet. Wrong again. It's really because the genius who designed them forgot that rubber shoes don't breathe, and Yankees who wear them for several years develop webbed toes from all the moisture.

One thing you must understand about Yankees is that when they eventually decide to brave the outdoors, it's only on the condition that they can bring as much of the insides of their homes with them as is humanly possible: pets, chairs, two or three chests of food, a complete medical kit, umbrellas, changes of costume, games for diversion (so they won't know they're outside), fifteen pairs of sunglasses, blankets, books, tents and awnings of all varieties, a bar for mixed drinks, paper towels, plates, baskets full of ointments, and insect foggers. This is for a day at the beach or an afternoon picnic; if the outing is to take several days, most Yankees need a trailer for their essential personal belongings. If you ask Northern friends to go fishing or swimming at the lake, figure on about three hundred pounds of equipment per Yankee per day.

Of course, if you're fortunate, you'll be able to invite a Californian along to balance the scales. Californians are into depravity in the name of environmental purity. Hence, they usually only show up with a little dried fruit, a compass, and some really smart mountaineering glasses with yellow lenses. One note of caution: Many West Coast Yankees have become physically ill, have recoiled in horror, at the littering habits of a single Southerner. The old "ashes to ashes, beer can to beer can" philosophy of most Southerners gives the average Californian convulsions, so try to distract them while you're ditching your Moon Pie wrappers.

THE SHORE

Most of the water in the North, whether in lakes or in the old North Atlantic, is cold. Very cold. Consequently, when Yankees think of "going to the shore," as they say, they usually have no intention of going any *further* than the shore; under no circumstances *in the* water. That's another reason they always take so many chairs and books and blankets and the like. Now, to the Southerner, taking the water away from the beach would leave very little reason to go. But Yankees have dreamed up thousands of diversions for their beach trips, including birdwatching, collecting driftwood, and forming nature clubs.

The king of all such Yankee diversions is the New England clambake. Entire weeks are spent planning for this big pig-out. Southerners have seen this sort of thing in hundreds of beer ads, but may nonetheless find it surprising to find there really *are* clambakes in the North. Originally, the main idea of a Yankee clambake was a harvest fresh from the sea, prepared and eaten after a day of fishing, crabbing, and clam digging. Of course, this could only be partaken of by folks who lived near the sea, mostly craggy, ruddy old New England fishermen and their wives, and this is not the stuff that makes great beer ads. In fact, most people who have clambakes with all the stuff that makes them picturesque as well as appetizing are usually lawyers out for a weekend. These people don't want to waste their time mucking about with a bunch of smelly fish, so most of the essentials are purchased from craggy, ruddy old fishermen early in the morning and stored in a securely anchored trap in the ocean until they are cooked. The truly lazy will drag their seafood in ice chests from the city and then quickly remove all the wrappers so that the guests will still comment on how fresh seafood can't be beat. Only God knows how many lobsters have been caught in Maine, transported to Boston,

THE SHORE

purchased in Newton, and then returned to the shore to be served as "fresh" to unsuspecting guests. The only satisfaction to the informed in this particular situation is the decadent appeal of knowing that over forty-five gallons of gasoline were used to bring this crustacean to the table. One note of caution: Never let lobsters that you've purchased in the city get a glance at the sea or they will start whining. This will upset the children.

Anyway, to run a clambake: Once you have your food in hand, the next thing to get is about half a cord of driftwood. If you don't find a good supply at hand, anything will do: packing crates, furniture, whatever. A true major-league production will also need rocks. What you do is build a monster fire on the rocks and then, when the fire has raged for an hour or two and all the rocks are hot, you add the food. If you are both rockless and driftwoodless, charcoal briquets do just as well (even if they do it less authentically). Place some seaweed on the rocks or coals, then pile all your food, starting with the "steamers" (or, as we call them, clams), on the seaweed in layers, with lobsters on top. Cover the whole mess with more seaweed and then with a large piece of heavy, wet canvas. Bury the edges of the canvas in the sand, sealing it, and have guests pour seawater over the canvas if it should start to dry out. The entire soggy pile becomes a steamer of sorts and will cook all the food, provided you haven't messed up the fire, in about an hour or so. This is obviously the slow, complex way of doing things.

Now, if you blow it, you will uncover the entire mess in front of fifty starving guests and have about a hundred pounds of warm, smelly, semi-alive fish parts. Not a pretty sight. The safer way to do a clambake is to go to a restaurant and arrange to have it cater the whole affair disguised as distant members of your family.

CRIME

There are countless numbers and types of crime in the North. Yankees actually invented almost all types of crime, with the exception of those Southern specialties, rustling, shooting, and stabbing. Below are a few of the biggies that you should be aware of when dealing with Yankees, especially on their home turf.

Murder. This is the one that requires the most creativity and has become exceedingly popular. For a while, people were pointing to Houston, Texas, as the murder capital, but they didn't think that one through. The reason for Houston's brief prominence was the massive influx of people from the North, who brought their penchant for murder with them. Now that they've begun to adapt to Southern ways, Houston no longer is plagued with violence. The interesting thing in the North is that even with strict handgun control, they still continue to snuff one another out, but with strange murder weapons. The only apparent achievement in controlling guns has been to force the locals to improvise, which they've done with typical Yankee ingenuity. It's not uncommon to open a newspaper and see that people have been murdered by ballpoint pens, bowling balls, gasoline, garden implements, attack hamsters, or flashlights.

The Mafia. How many crimes is the Mafia behind? Who knows? If they do know, who talks? The Sicilians brought art, and a gift for metaphor, to the unpleasantries. They coined such household phrases as "concrete overcoat," "heater," "brass knuckles," the "big sleep," "early retirement," and others. They brought us the rackets, the numbers, loan sharks. They introduced the Thompson machine gun as a negotiating tool. Naturally, it's tough maintaining the image, and heavy losses in direct confrontations with the Feds have made a number of the large families diversify and keep much lower profiles as of late. Still, you can't keep a good family down, and even the Mob has been moving south. Las Vegas was a big step, followed most recently by Florida. However, it's different in the South, and Mafiosi stick out like sore thumbs in most parts, especially those wearing trenchcoats. Another problem relocated mobsters face is the unlimited amount of weapons available in the South, along with the local predilection for vigilante justice. Hence, moving into an area can be a little tougher since it's always hard selling protection to a man with an automatic weapon.

Heating Oil Theft. This is a relative newcomer, but it just goes to show how ingenious those Yanks are. First of all, Southerners should know that in many parts of the North, furnaces are fired with heating oil, which is purchased by the gallon, much like gasoline. The way to easy profits is to lease or buy a tank truck, get some rigged papers, drive up to a loading station, and pump yourself thirty or forty thousand gallons. There is absolutely NO problem selling the stuff.

Mugging. The classic, and very embarrassing on first dates.

Over-Cooking Steaks. The North's number one crime against nature. Fear of the unknown is the culprit responsible for this heinous practice, plus a woeful attraction to tasteless food. Often, Southerners are forced to leave restaurants in tears after watching a sequence of well-done sirloins pass by their tables.

Wharf Rats. Resembling dogs rather than mice, wharf rats can take the groceries away from anything that weighs less than a hundred pounds. It's a definite mistake to take your lunch to the pier unless you want to share. Natives of the docks have solved the problem by trapping the rats, bobbing their tails, and selling them as pets in outlying areas. This accounts for the large number of strange looking terriers found in parts of Connecticut and New Hampshire.

Bomber Pigeons. A winged version of the toy poodle, these creatures are totally without redeeming social value. Perched atop buildings and monuments, they calculatingly select their targets based on how new the clothes, how inopportune the occasion, and how many people are around to witness the event. Then with deadly accuracy they swoop, dropping their payload and cackling wildly. Most visitors believe that Northerners carry umbrellas because of the rain. Locals know better.

Landsharks. A broad group including, but not limited to, real-estate agents, literary agents, and maître d's. Once they perceive that they stand between you and something you need, their dorsal fin starts emerging. They can smell fear and insecurity, and during the last moments of an attack you will notice their eyes will roll back in their heads and they will operate strictly on instinctual homing. Never go into a landshark-infested area without negotiable securities or cash to fend them off with.

Toy Poodles. Poodles, especially the toy variety, are acknowledged to defecate an amount equal to their own weight every two days. In cities this increases from lack of exercise. This problem was all but eliminated in the South when hunting season on the little brutes was first opened.

Sleeping Bums. Nothing will take the edge off an evening like emerging from a classy restaurant and tripping over a street sleeper. Better still is to find one in your elevator. Street bums can sense, even in a deep stupor, when people are present and will start to moan or get sick the moment you come close to them. This is their defense mechanism, similar to porcupines' use of their quills.

Esoteric sports run rampant in the North. Here's a random sampling:

Softball. Every area in the North seems to have its own variety of softball, but there are a couple of especially noteworthy versions that deserve mention. First, Chicago Ball. This is your basic softball except that it's played without gloves and with a ball that has a sixteen-inch circumference (as opposed to the regular eleven-inch). This monster ball requires a good pop to go over the fence, and Chicago Ball players usually are all powerful hitters named Stan who have large flat hands with webbed fingers. Another most unusual version, played at the City Athletic Club in New York, is Indoor Ball. This is played on a much smaller, hardwood field with high walls in a gymnasium. The ball is rubber-coated, and it's legal to catch it as it bounces off the walls. It's a fast game and one that is seldom rained out.

Lacrosse. The dry-land version of hockey, it's played primarily along the East Coast, and even the South has a few states in which lacrosse can be found. The object of the game is to put the ball in a goal located at each end. This is done by tossing it man-to-man with a stick attached to a small net. Honest.

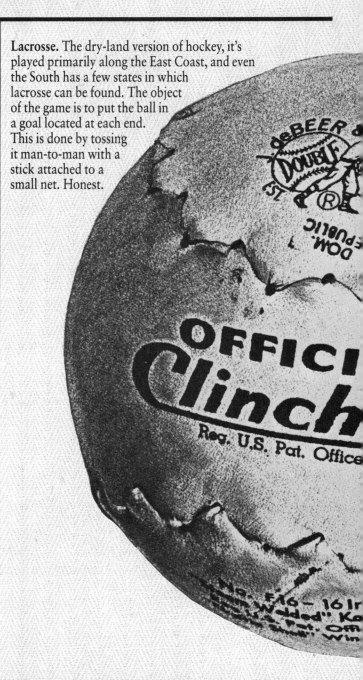

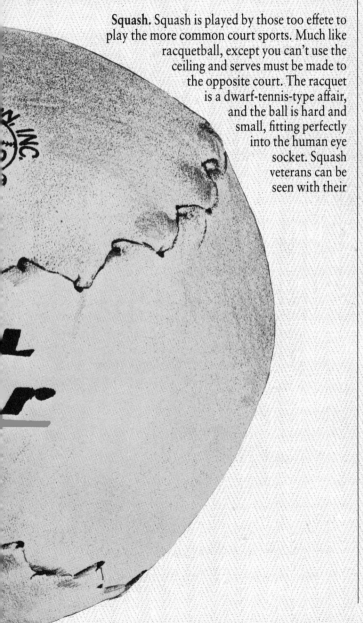

Squash. Squash is played by those too effete to play the more common court sports. Much like racquetball, except you can't use the ceiling and serves must be made to the opposite court. The racquet is a dwarf-tennis-type affair, and the ball is hard and small, fitting perfectly into the human eye socket. Squash veterans can be seen with their dogs and white canes in front of racquet clubs throughout the East.

Hockey. The primary Yankee sport. Southerners know very little about hockey, since it requires a lot of ice and doesn't televise well. Some Southerners, in fact, will watch two or three hockey games before they discover the puck. The idea is to put the puck in the opposing goal while injuring as many members of the other team as you can. Good players are judged by how subtly they can inflict injury: Gordie Howe, for instance, appeared to have people fainting all around him as he skated casually across the ice.

Hockey is about as close as modern man gets to gladiator-style sports and, consequently, makes a great spectator event, with the fans often erupting into wanton fights and abuse. The key word to know in hockey is "check"; it describes hitting anything except the puck.

RELIGION

A hundred years ago, the North teemed with its very own religious sects. Unfortunately, a large number of the more bizarre and interesting ones have slowly faded away due to their inflexible nature and an ill-founded penchant for beliefs and creeds. Still, a few remain.

New England Congregationalists. In almost every small New England town you will find a group of these. Congregationalists love the idea of church, religious architecture, and bake sales. It's religion itself they don't care much for. They are a very social and gregarious group, and hardly a weekend goes by during the summer without some sort of event or fete.

Congregational sermons vary from church to church, and some of the most incisive and revealing book reviews in modern history have come from certain of their pulpits.

Amish. The Amish are the North's leading "back to nature" group. Their idea of fun is to live their lives as much as possible in the style of the earliest Christians. This makes for interesting conflict with the twentieth century. For instance, things that modern man takes for granted, like zippers, don't figure into the Amish existence. Other things that don't fit into their existence are can openers, stereos, automobiles, digital computers, and automatic weapons. Amish wear clothes that are terribly out of fashion and they seldom go to discos.

Mennonites. These are a more joyful, fun-loving version of the Amish. While they still are leery of machinery, they will occasionally use it provided it's not too flashy. A Mennonite automobile may have all its chrome painted black, for instance. Mennonites are also noted for making extremely good food, even without food processors.

Catholics. There are many places in the South where you can grow up, age, and die without ever meeting a Catholic. In the North, however, you can't escape them. Everywhere you look, there's another Catholic building. They're sort of the Southern Baptists of the North, except that Catholics throw much better parties. And lots more of them. This gives everyone something to confess: "Forgive me, Father, I was at your party last night." This tradition continues right up until (and after) you die. The final party is called a "wake"; it requires the neighbors to do so often.

Quakers. The organization is actually called the Society of Friends, but they are known as Quakers because they're crazy about oats. There are several types of Quakers, as each Quaker is encouraged to interpret the Bible personally; the Eighteen-Minute Society of Believers was founded by lifelong Quaker Richard Nixon just before he left office in 1974.

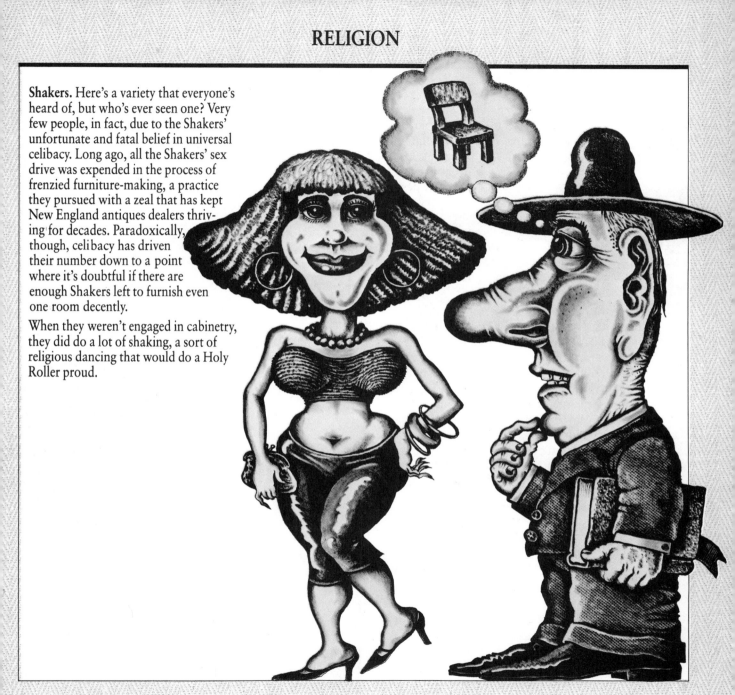

Shakers. Here's a variety that everyone's heard of, but who's ever seen one? Very few people, in fact, due to the Shakers' unfortunate and fatal belief in universal celibacy. Long ago, all the Shakers' sex drive was expended in the process of frenzied furniture-making, a practice they pursued with a zeal that has kept New England antiques dealers thriving for decades. Paradoxically, though, celibacy has driven their number down to a point where it's doubtful if there are enough Shakers left to furnish even one room decently.

When they weren't engaged in cabinetry, they did do a lot of shaking, a sort of religious dancing that would do a Holy Roller proud.

KETCHUP

In the South, ketchup is used for only three things: french fries, onion rings, and shrimp. That's as it should be. In the North, however, you will find ketchup abuse to be rampant. Ketchup still remains the spiciest seasoning that many Yankees ever encounter. Consequently, they have a habit of using it on everything. Each day, thousands of gallons of ketchup are poured over perfectly good steaks. Hamburger chains in the North use it shamelessly. In some places, you even have to request that it *not* be used or you will find yourself eating a tomato burger. Even more disgusting is the practice of using ketchup as a substitute for BBQ sauce.

If you are having a dinner party with Yankees present, chances are they are suffering Ketchup Withdrawal and at some point during the meal, regardless of what you are serving, they will ask for some of the stuff. To save the rest of the guests from having to watch the spectacle of a grown man pouring ketchup over a medium-rare prime rib, many Southern hostesses erect a small partition around the plate of any ketchup user. This keeps the rest of your dinner party from becoming enraged or violently ill.

STREET FOOD

Only Mexico can boast of anywhere close to the number of street food vendors that lurk in the North. Basically, anything that can be eaten can be bought somewhere in the North from a street vendor. Vendor food has a certain efficient appeal, and urban Yankees will suffer withdrawal symptoms if forced away from it for very long. Vendor food also allows many to spend their lunch hours browsing in shops or reading, thus enriching their lives and keeping restaurants less crowded. It's easy to see why Yankees value such fare so much.

True vendor food is dispensed by a one-man operation. The entire mess is usually contained in an umbrella-covered pushcart whose operator prepares, cooks, hawks, and serves the product. Here are some of the more common vendors that inhabit the North:

Weenie Wagons. A standard fixture on street corners, particularly in the Northeast. Elaborate operations will have soft drinks and a choice of relishes in addition to the dogs. (In Chicago, many vendors offer the potent firedog; in Milwaukee, a "Polish" is a spicy sausage, not an ethnic joke.) Once you've decided on which dog you want, the next big choice is kraut or no kraut. This can be an important decision, and seasoned veterans always have a look at the kraut before requesting any. Extremely upper level establishments provide grease-proof napkins and Bromo. (Note: When possible, rely on kosher dogs. This will protect you from some of the seamier practices of the meat-packing industry.)

Nut Wagons. Most offer a number of products, but almost all carry chestnuts, peanuts, and soft pretzels. Unfortunately, nut wagons are always manned by people who look like criminals from another country, and this has scared away most of the glitter trade from the carts.

Caviar Stands. The familiar cry is heard in metropolises from Wilmington to Eau Claire: "Bloogaba, bloogaba, gitcher bloogahea" ("Beluga bar, beluga bar, get your beluga here"). The stands, in years past invariably the property of the North's immense Iranian population, are now dominated by recently arrived Kurdish émigrés.

Ice Cream Carts. There are a number of different frozen products available from vendors. Italian ice is the biggie in a lot of Northern cities, appearing in such flavors as lemon, chocolate, raspberry, and, in some neighborhoods, garlic. Less ethnic cities feature Good Humor carts, which specialize in fifteen-cent ice cream bars at seventy-five cents each.

Shish Kebabs. When they're great, they simply are unbeatable. When they're bad, you will spend a few days in the hospital. The main thing is trying to figure out what meat is being used and how many days it has been cooking. Far-sighted owners usually make sure that the vendor speaks only Armenian, making the experience of getting a good shish kebab more visual than verbal. If a barking dog causes the vendor to flinch, take a closer look.

DISCOVERING AN ITALIAN RESTAURANT

This is a favorite pastime of Yankees. It's also a favorite of Italian restaurant owners. No matter how many good Italian restaurants any Yankee knows about, there's always that strange, unquenchable desire to find another. Of course, any good Italian restaurant entrepreneur recognizes that it would be suicidal to make his establishment comfortable and highly visible, and thereby deprive his potential clientele of the thrill of the hunt. Here are a few pointers so you'll know how to distinguish a great obscure Italian restaurant from the average variety.

The line waiting for tables should extend out the front door, up some stairs, and onto the sidewalk. This is especially true in the winter or during rain storms.

Tables should be no more than eighteen inches from one another, forcing everyone in the restaurant to rise when anyone has to go to the bathroom. Of course, there should be no bathrooms.

For some reason, almost all good Italian restaurants fall into two categories: those where a plate of fettucine costs less than $2.50 and those where a plate of fettucine costs more than $18.

The owner should always be angry, bitch at the waiters, and act short (some would say rude) with the patrons.

There should be rumors of at least one celebrity dining there recently. (A photo of the owner and Dick Cavett embracing will suffice.)

One table should have customers from an Arab country. That will be the table with all the waiters around it.

The time that it takes to order, be served, eat, and pay your bill should be either less than thirty minutes or more than three hours.

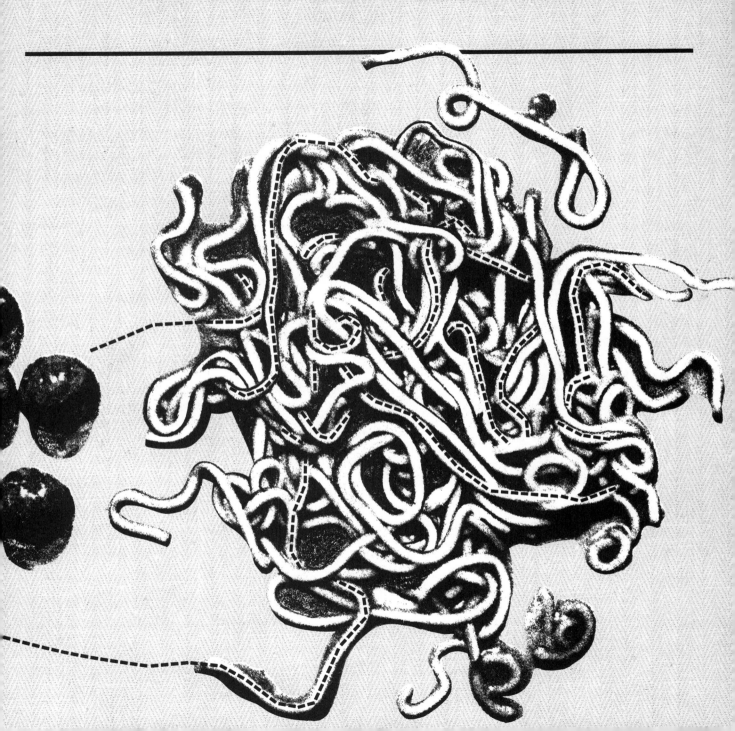

DRINKING IN THE NORTH

Of the several things that a Southerner should understand before going North or spending much time with Yankees, one of the most important is the Yankee drinking habit. God knows there is no shortage of liquor in the South, but Southerners tend towards binging, whereas Yankees are always a little bit drunk. Drinking is really more of a profession in the North than an entertainment, and even the casual observer will note that what Yankees lack in style they more than make up for in sheer quantity. Here are some pointers:

Mixed Drinks. Generally speaking, Southerners take their liquor straight. Not so in the North. They love mixed drinks. Any mixed drink. Most Yankees would prefer a drink mixed with anything (rubbing alcohol, Elmer's glue, beet juice) to drinking something straight from the bottle. That's why it's extremely rare to find a Northern household that doesn't have at least two blenders. It's considered a point of honor that the host should be able to produce an excellent version of absolutely any drink that you might want from the bar stock that he has on hand. Next to a home and automobile, the bar stock is the largest average family expenditure in the North. Northerners are also big on stylistic matters, such as not bruising the ice.

Martini Lunch. The martini is just about as close as Yankees will ever get to a real, straight drink. Basically gin, with a touch of vermouth and an indeterminate number of olives, the martini is the fundamental of all urban drinking. If you have occasion to do business in almost any major city in the North, you will doubtless encounter what is cleverly called the Martini Lunch. *Don't be confused by the term "lunch."* The food part is entirely optional, and usually forgotten in the course of drinking. A great number of contracts have been routinely signed after such a "lunch" by Southerners who were in the waning stages of consciousness. Don't be so easily taken in. Prepare for those trips with a rigorous training program. When you can knock down five or ten martinis with little effect, you should consider yourself ready.

Boilermakers. These come direct from the factories of Pittsburgh, a town that will make even the stout of heart turn to something substantial in the way of refreshment. In a normal world, one might imagine that the logical way to drink whiskey and beer would be mixed together in advance, or one following the other. Wrong. Here's how it's done: You take a full stein of beer and drop your shotglass full of whiskey, bottom down, into it. Next, after a moment's pause, you glug the whole thing down, banzai-style. Rudimentary logic will alert you to the distinct possibility of swallowing a couple of shot glasses before the night is over, but then that's what they call gusto in some parts of the North. You can gain immediate acceptance in many bars by chewing up and swallowing your shotglass.

DRINKING IN THE NORTH

DELI FOOD

The North enjoyed a rich addition to its cuisine when the Eastern European Jews hit Manhattan. Their greatest contribution to American culture was the delicatessen; just as a Southerner will drive a hundred miles to get some good BBQ, Yankees will go to extremes for good deli food. Unfortunately, the South was slow in acquiring a Jewish population, and, consequently, there were few delis there until after World War II. Astonishing as it may seem to many Yankees, Southerners have been salami- and bagel-starved until very recent times, and in some southern cities delis are as rare as chitlins at a bar mitzvah. The deli is one of the few things worth having that Yankees who move South will bring with them, so don't miss out.

Delicatessens have two parts. The counter (you will find inferior imitations in some of the hipper Southern supermarkets) and the restaurant (hard to find even bad imitations south of Philadelphia). A very few good full-service delicatessens in the South already await you, so some key items you might want to familiarize yourself with are described here. It's important to learn to say these words very quickly, preferably with a scowl on your face, if you expect anything close to good service.

DELI FOOD

Knish. The basic potato dumpling. Extremely good and best ordered in small quantities, unless you don't intend to eat again during the same month. The traditional hot mustard that is served with them is weird, but tasty. Don't be a hopeless cracker and ask for ketchup: The knish is not simply a gigantic french fry and shouldn't be treated like one.

Bagel. The Hope Diamond of all deli breads. Sort of like an extremely dense doughnut without the sugar. Be sure to slice horizontally; vertically cut bagels hold very little cream cheese.

Lox. Smoked salmon. Its many varieties include: from the rivers of eastern Canada, Nova Scotia lox; from the Pacific Northwest, Columbia River lox; and from New Haven, Connecticut, Yale lox.

Stuffed Derma. Intestines filled with some kind of mush. Like they say at Taco Bell, "It tastes as good as it looks."

Egg Cream. Seltzer (what we call club soda) with a little milk and a little chocolate sauce. It contains neither eggs nor cream and might just as accurately be called "broccoli butter."

Matzoh Ball Soup. Dough-like balls simmered in chicken broth. Used to cure everything from colds to cancer; two bowls and you'll be as good as new.

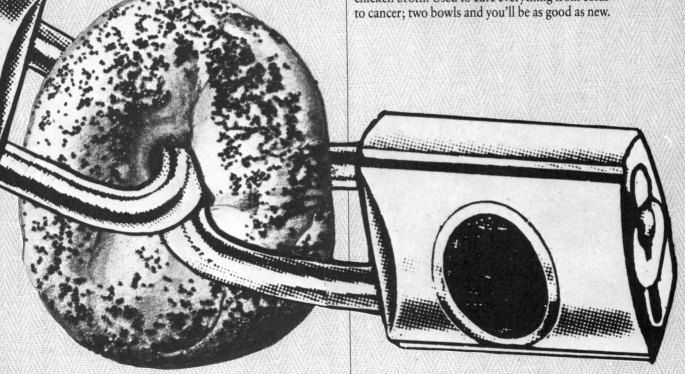

Yankees new to the South may be witnessed during their first several weeks here driving around looking for a diner. It's natural and should be tolerated. What they are missing can't really be found in the South for many reasons, but primarily because Southerners know what they want. Diners were created for those who don't. They specialize in creating hundreds of dishes. If you suddenly are struck with the feeling that you are in desperate need of eggs, rutabagas, and kosher pickles, then a diner is the place for you. Any good one will have at least five dishes with those ingredients.

Most diners operate without regard to the hour of the day and will gladly give you waffles with a side order of carrots and some chocolate cake at seven in the morning, or ten in the evening. Other diners have abandoned menus altogether, since it gets to be an expensive proposition printing all the five hundred or so dishes that any decent diner will specialize in.

Silvertop Diners. One of the few examples of recycling that can be found in the North. Most are made from old railroad dining cars and consist of one long counter with stools facing the grill. Often these are Ma and Pa operations, which is a good sign because it means Ma and Pa have to eat there, too. Some of the more elaborate versions are enclosed by great stainless-steel walls and are terrific to look at. This is convenient because at many of them you should only look; eating can be a big mistake.

Greek Diners. Somehow, diners run by other nationalities just don't feel right. A good Greek diner will prepare all five hundred of its entrées in the same grease. People who go to diners are expected to be forgiving types, so don't send the food back unless there's something alive in it. Greek diners are one reason that Yankees usually prefer to cook very bland, safe food at home, and a week of diner food will make even a Southerner see some wisdom in their logic.

Geek Diners. These are run by ethnic groups of indeterminate origin—Poles, Newfoundlanders, Stumpies, and the like. You can tell when you are in one immediately: They will be out of the first three things you order. Usually, they only cook two or three items and sell them under several names. Don't be surprised if your dish of beef Stroganoff looks quite like the next guy's Irish stew. The attraction of geek diners is the arguing among the help. Yankees feel better if they know the people around them are bitter and contentious.

FINAL EXAM

Answer these correctly and you are
eligible to spend a week in Syracuse.

1. What do L. L. Bean's initials
   stand for?
2. What is tomalley?
3. What is an antique?
4. Why do Yankees speak with a
   Southern accent on the CB radio?
5. What is a drumette and why do
   Yankees like them?

5. *Smaller than a drum major and fried. Who knows?*
4. *When in Rome. . . .*
3. *Anything older than your grandmother.*
2. *Nasty green lobster liver.*
1. *Large Lima.*

1. *Sixteen to twenty-three, depending on the size (of the teeth).*

2. *Mosquito netting.*

3. *It depends on what they have done. If they've been real bad, send them to their room for twenty-four to forty-eight hours.*

4. *No one knows, but at least three hundred if all who have claimed the relation are to be believed.*

5. *Tiny shoes made out of corn meal. The ultimate sole food.*

FINAL EXAM

Answer these and win admission to Auburn.

1. How many teeth are alloted to the average hillbilly family?
2. What is the primary use for tire chains in the South?
3. How do you cure hams?
4. How many brothers does Chuck Berry have?
5. What are hush puppies?

KEEPING WARM

A cold Yankee with a chainsaw is a dangerous thing to have around if you like woods or trees. Come August, most get a glint in their eyes and start looking for combustible material. Then, much like busy beavers, the ritual of building the firewood stack begins. The South's mild winters often fool first-time residents, and many will continue sawing right through to April in anticipation of a freak blizzard. A few years of this behavior and you have a dilemma. What does a person do with more than four hundred cords of wood? This explains why many Yankees become such avid barbequers. Others, in the final throes of serious fire withdrawal, will put the central air conditioning on fifty degrees in a last ditch effort to produce a climate that demands a roaring fire. Thus, the concept of reverse ignition was born.

A delicate process at best, reverse ignition is the best way to light a fire in an air-conditioned house. Trial and error is the only way to perfect the technique, but for those in chronic need of fire, reverse ignition is the only way to get a wood stove going during the spring, summer, or fall months.

First, turn the air conditioning down all the way and start rounding up ice.

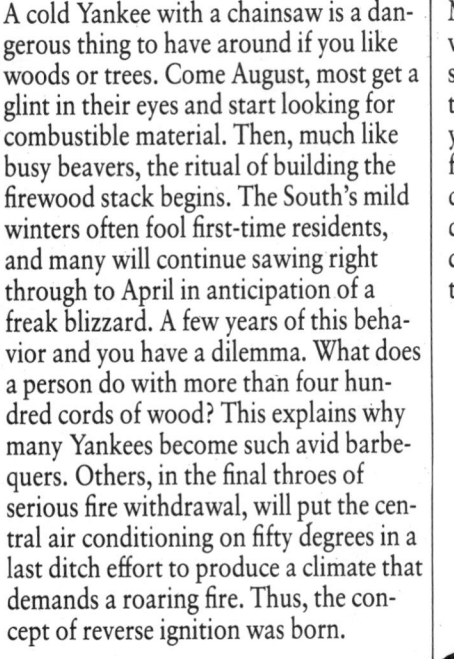

Meanwhile, soak some beach towels in water. When it starts getting frosty inside your house, quickly get a ladder, take the ice up on the roof, and pack your wood stove's smokestack. This is for later. Now rush down, put the kindling in the firebox, and, with the damper *closed*, light your fire. Open the damper just a little to let oxygen get to the fledgling fire. The outside temperature will always be warmer than the inside air, thus oxygen will always come *in* from the stack. The trick is to get the fire going well enough to warm the air and create an upward draft without smoking up the entire house as more air rushes *down* the stack. That's where the wet beach towels come in. Wrap them around the stove, leaving only a hole for your arm to play with the fire. If successfully executed, the fire will build quickly, the towels will contain the smoke in the first critical minutes, and when the thing is going good, snapping the damper open will reverse the draft (the ice will have by this time cooled the air in the stack) and your fire will spring to life.

If the fire starts too slowly, or you bungle the technique, be prepared for a houseful of cool black smoke and a lot of ribbing from your neighbors. You might be asking yourself, why not simply turn the air conditioning off and wait until the inside temperature is warmer than the outside? Well, old timers will tell you that it's hard, even for a Yankee, to enjoy sitting in a 120-degree house in front of a raging fire. Besides, you couldn't wear your sweater and drink hot toddies.

SOUTHERN PESTS

Gulf Mosquito. A large-sized version of the Northern species. Gulf mosquito bites are measured in pints, and repeated bites can cause anemia in the very young. One should be cautious of slapping a full-grown Gulf mosquito, as the blood will stain a large area rug and completely ruin a formal dress.

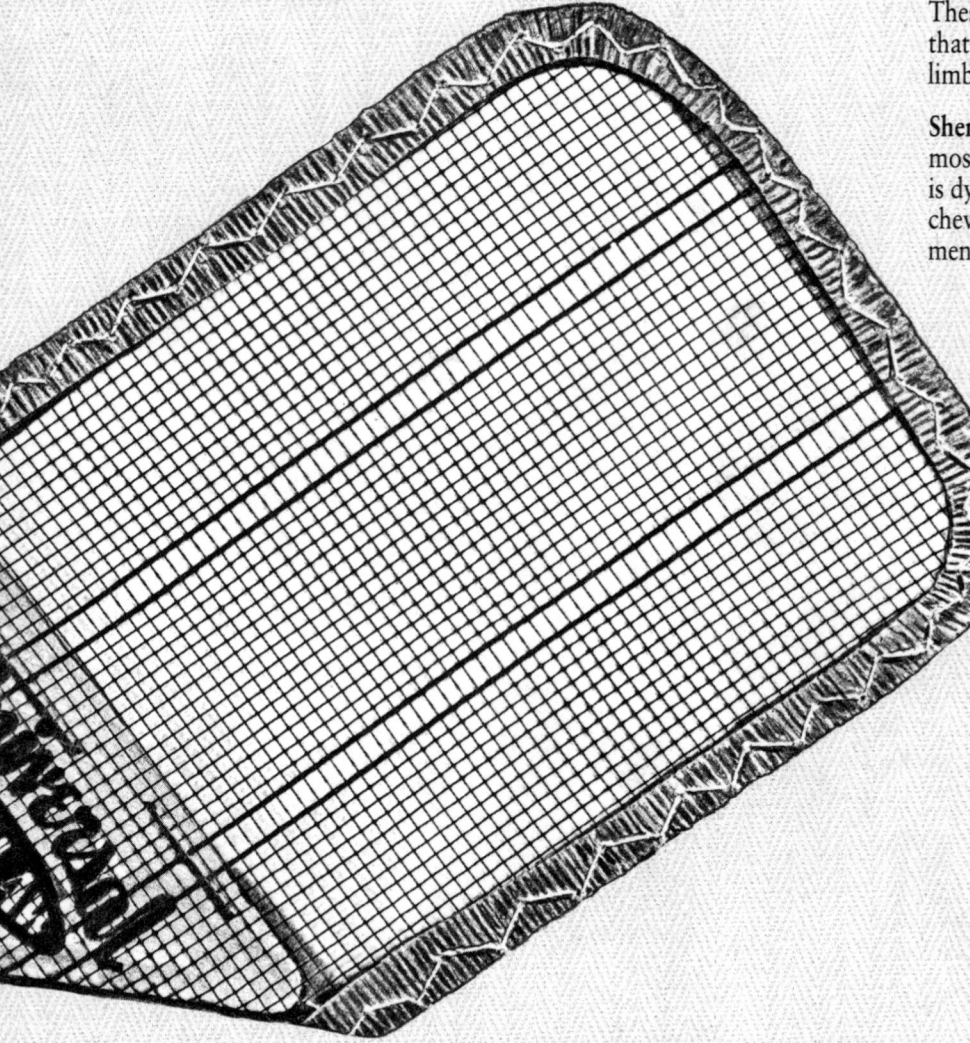

Bull Yellow Jackets. Nothing can put the fear of God in an otherwise courageous man quicker than a few hundred of these brutes. Even one enraged yellow jacket is something to contend with. These fist-sized predators deliver a sting that has been described as similar to limb amputation without anesthetic.

Sheriffs. The small-town variety is the most tiresome. Fortunately, the species is dying out—the victim of cigars, chewing tobacco, and too many complimentary meals.

SOUTHERN PESTS

Southern Roach. Few Yankees have seen anything as large and prehistoric-looking as the Southern roach. Between four and seven inches in length, the bulls are able to run at over thirty-five mph. Keeping them out of your house is simple if you keep your doors and windows shut, stamp your feet loudly each time you enter your house, and toss tear-gas canisters into your kitchen every few days.

Coons. The raccoon is among the more formidable household pests in the South. It combines the curiosity of a cat with the digital dexterity of a monkey. Consequently, there is nothing that it cannot get into. Raccoons love to empty containers and go through whatever is inside. Sugar canisters, cigarette packs, garbage cans, and hope chests are particularly popular.

Many newcomers think that coon-hunting is a cruel sport, but after having had your house tossed a few times, you'll be more than ready to rip the lungs out of a few of the little pranksters.

Cottonmouths. An inhabitant of virtually all watery confines in the South, the cottonmouth (also called the water moccasin) is a venomous, vile creature with an extremely limited sense of humor. On top of everything else, it has a repugnant odor that will, at least, warn nonsmokers of its presence. Don't play with these unless you are within walking distance of a hospital.

Armadillos. These dim, harmless creatures have slowly worked their way across the entire South. Though heavily armored, the 'dillo is a deceptively adroit swimmer and can float by pumping up its stomach and intestines. Inveterate rooters, armadillos are extremely nearsighted and will actually root right under your feet if you let them. Their psychotic desire to ram automobiles has resulted in the common highway spectacle of 'dillo on the halfshell.

INSTRUMENTS

Dobro. Looks like a weird guitar with a chrome sound box. The dobro emits a metallic, lyrical hum often likened to what robots would sound like if they could sing.

Spoons. Generally considered percussion instruments without rival. Using them in soup before a concert tends to deaden the sound, unless you're a conscientious licker.

Jugs. As everyone knows, jugs come in all sizes and shapes. In the South, as elsewhere, most folks prefer large jugs, but a competent jug player will play all sizes. Start by blowing softly on the top to find your tone.

Juice Harp. Erroneously called the Jew's harp, this instrument is actually named for the spittle that will run down your chin while playing it.

Banjo. This is the biggie: The banjo is to Southern music what lemons are to lemonade. However, crabby types think the banjo is to Southern music what the Memphis phone book is to the art of reading; that is, boring in a painful sort of way.

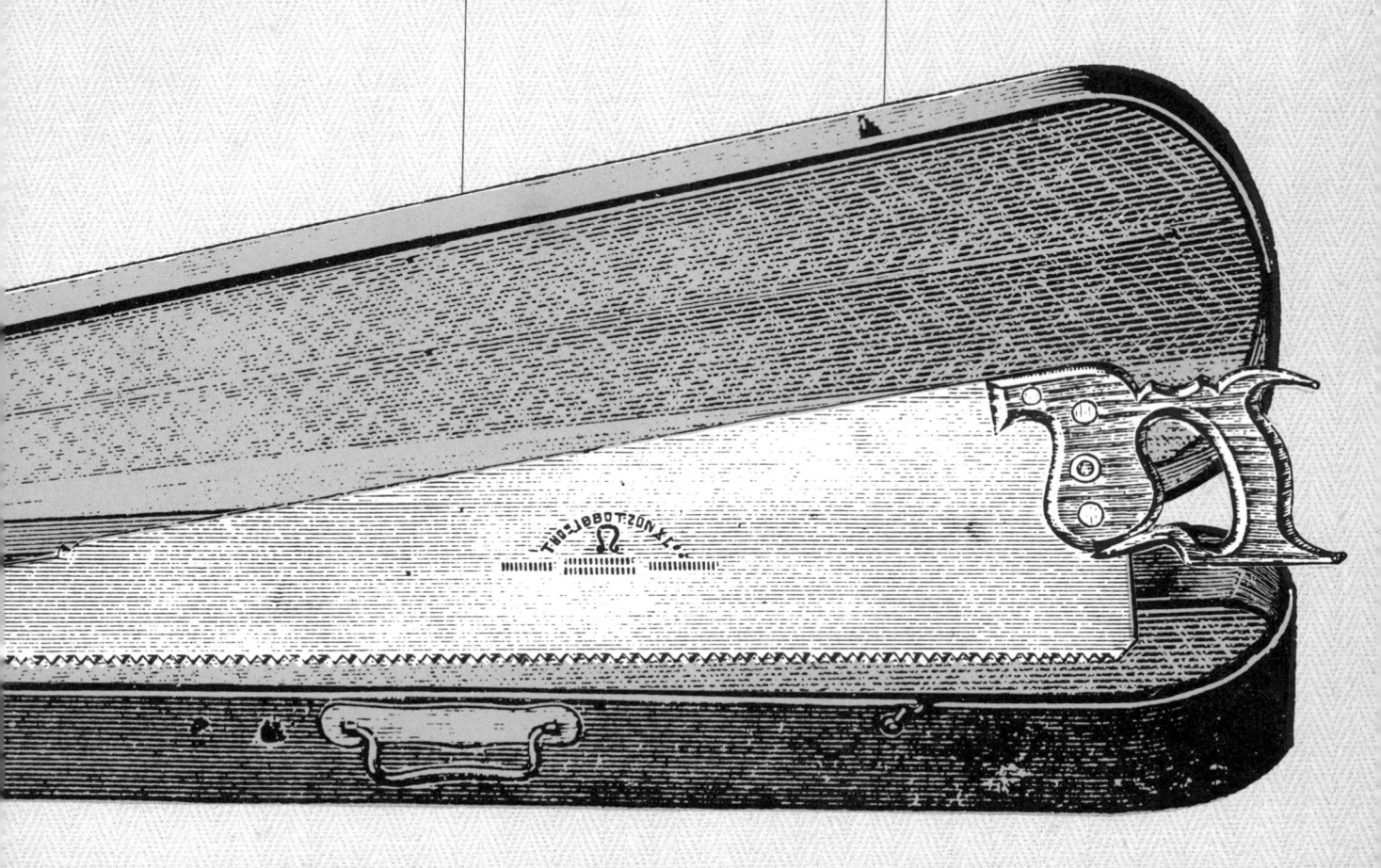

INSTRUMENTS

A zest for music, coupled with the region's historic poverty, has led to the creation of a host of native instruments in the South. No other section of this or any other country has invented so many different ways to make noise. Here are a few of those you are likely to encounter, but don't let that limit you. Vast research here has shown that almost any item can be manipulated to make music. If you want to play the Weed Eater, go for it.

Saw. Many are surprised when they first hear the siren-like song of the saw. An accomplished player can get more than an octave out of an ordinary wood saw, but a rare and awesome sight to behold is two professional cedar-choppers playing the bass tree saw. The massive amplification that has influenced popular music since the 1960s has recently led to the rise of chainsaw virtuosos in parts of northern Louisiana.

Washtub Bass. Standard with many bluegrass bands, the washtub bass is easily manufactured by rigging a large tub with a broomhandle and some heavy string. There is little that compares to the gut-throbbing thumps of a well-played washtub bass. Newcomers will notice musicians in hardware stores softly thumping the bottoms of all manner of tubs and pails in their ongoing effort to discover one with the perfect acoustics.

Dulcimer. A lute-like instrument with infinite variations in sound due to its handmade origins and the consequent great variety of sound holes. The dulcimer comes in two types: the plucked string version, which is somewhat like a violin, and the hammered dulcimer, which is played with little sticks, vibes-style. Either one can create a sound that will make lovers' hearts throb and dogs' ears wiggle.

Washboard. Nothing beats the clacking rhythm of a vintage washboard played by a pro. This is a marginal instrument, however, and there's a thin line between incredible percussion effects and mere noise. The main problem for washboard players is keeping a sincere look during the solos. Practice the washboard with water and soap and get your clothes cleaned free in the process.

Zither. Basically, a lap instrument with a fingerboard and twenty to forty strings. Before you start counting your fingers, remember that most of the zither's strings are sympathetic strings; this is handy, because zither players often need all the sympathy they can get.

Bones. Usually rib bones, these are played like spoons. You have to eat a lot of hogs to get the right bones, hence there are very few bone players that weigh less than three hundred pounds. It just goes to show that something good can come from playing with your food.

For the urban shopper, the challenge is to find a use for what's there. Watering tanks make wonderful planters or casual tables, for instance. And there is always an ample supply of funky clothing. You will be pleasantly surprised to find that most clothing bought at a feedstore is the variety that lasts and lasts, so don't be too cavalier in choosing something. A good feedstore will also usually sell some local produce, often traded for merchandise by a local farmer. The bartering system is still alive in the country, and once you establish a relationship with the proprietor, there is virtually no limit to what will be considered in trade. Here are a few items that are "musts" for your feedstore shopping list:

Gimme Caps. An essential. Don't be fooled into buying one of the imitation varieties available at convenience stores. Get a real, authentic one from the feedstore. "Certified Seeds," or something like that, should be printed on the front. Stay away from anything that has a beer or truck manufacturer's logo. "Purina" is always a good one.

Eggs. Not the clean, white variety. Feedstore eggs should be brown, speckled, and have straw stuck to the outsides.

Floursacks or Seedsacks. Nothing is as good for pajamas as a soft cotton flour or seed sack. They also have that appealing smell.

Checkered Shirts. In the feedstore you will find that rural America welcomes all the new fabrics that don't wear out. Try and get a Western-cut, snap-version shirt. You'll find that most are tailored for stubby people, so make sure that the arms are long enough, and plan on gaining a lot of weight for the proper fit.

Fencing Tool. A great item. It's the Swiss Army knife of farmers and ranchers—a combination hammer, pliers, wire cutter, and pick that has a lot of other uses after you study the thing for a while. No one should be without a couple.

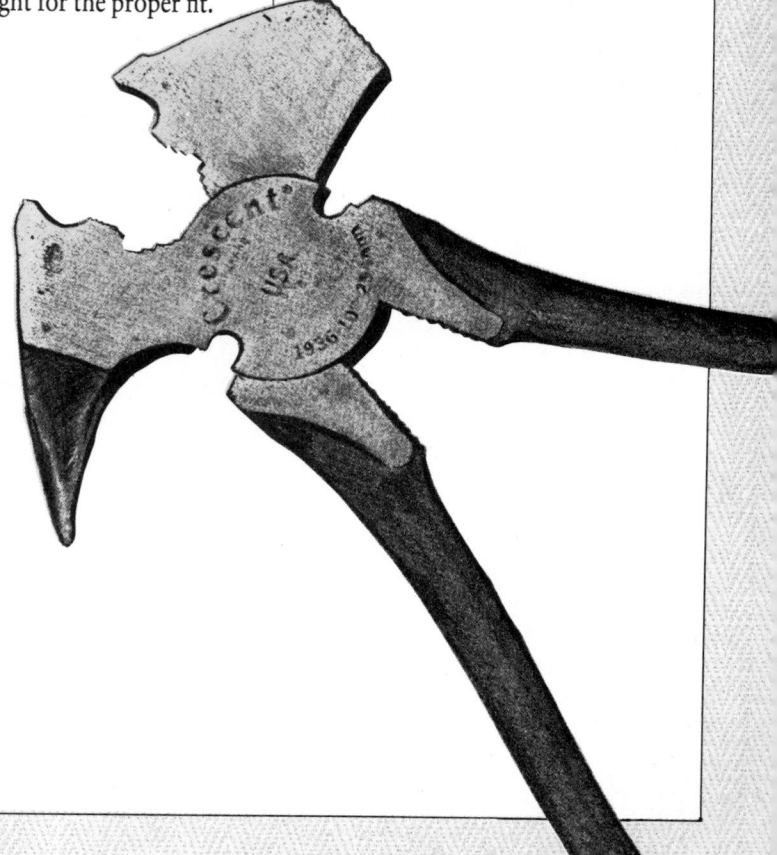

Few retail institutions can surpass a good feedstore for both the usefulness and variety of their products. Feedstores appear all over the South, and they are often the center of the community in the smaller towns. If you are unfortunate enough to live in a city, then you should make a point of finding a good feedstore a few miles out in the country.

At a feedstore there is always something you need; the trick is finding it. To prevent the management from thinking that you are a dilettante, you should always have something in mind when the clerk asks if you need help. There are many items that will qualify, since feedstores have the combined attraction of satisfying both the hardware lust and the clothing need. Hats, shirts, tools, chicken feeders, seeds of all varieties . . . you name it and they probably have it.

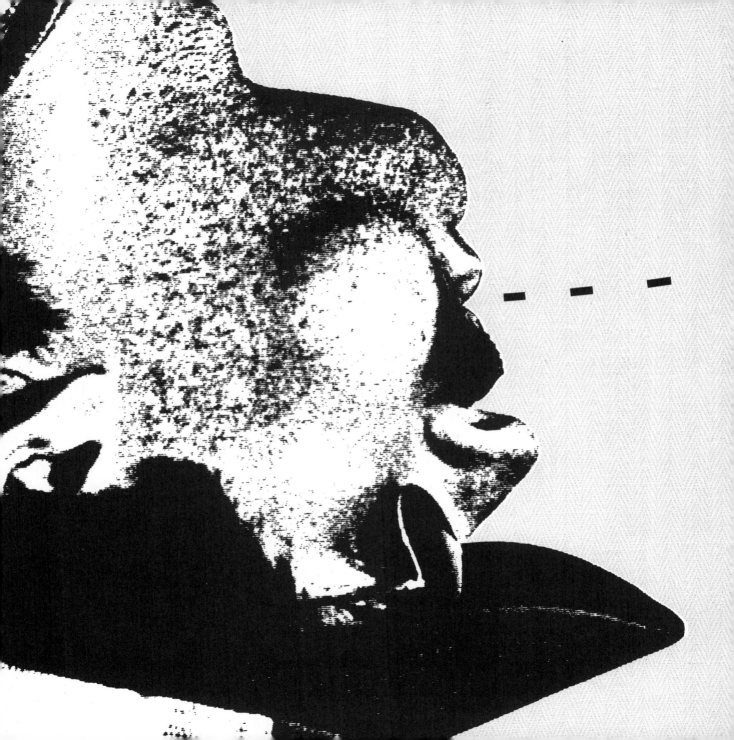

CHEWING TOBACCO

Chewing tobacco is a vile, disgusting habit. Let's get that right out front. But as a certain number (about half) of all Southerners have an abiding attraction for things vile and disgusting, massive amounts of tobacco are chewed in the South. Learning to chew is considered by many (especially Yankees) as the final step in a person's Southernization; once you chew, you can never again even pretend to be from Connecticut.

The true traditional chaw is plug tobacco. This is a tightly packed brick, and a knife is required to cut a chaw from the plug. If you carry a knife at all times, as many Southerners do, then you might as well go for the basic and deal with plug tobacco only. Precut, or looseleaf, tobacco is taken in a bunch and squeezed together just before chewing, or stuffed salad-style into your mouth and bunched together there. All you have to do from this point is chew. Many people find they have to build up to chewing, so you always warm up by munching a few packs of Picayunes or maybe a cigar or two.

When you finally have the chewing down, and know how to settle properly a load between your cheek and gums, you need to get your style down. A big part of style is constantly looking around for the next place you're going to spit. This gives one the appearance of always being mildly distracted or introspective. Sometimes it's even confused with deep thought. A well-timed spit will further this image. Southern sheriffs have mastered the art of using tobacco to punctuate remarks and exclamations on a host of subjects. "So my deputy told him he could either mind his manners (SPLURT) *or find hisself a new ass.*" The trick is in the delivery. These sheriffs know that a short joke or anecdote can always be enhanced by leading the listener to the end, then spitting just before delivering the punch line. A longer tale will usually have several spits, the first immediately following the prelude: "Well, it all began last week when Daddy's hog ate little Luke (SPIT)...."

Another reason for the popularity of chewing tobacco in the South is fire prevention. It's a proven fact that farmers who smoke cigars while working have a much higher incidence of crop fires. Also, a hot ash carelessly flicked out of a pickup window can set your load of hay ablaze. Also, four or five farmers chewing tobacco can usually extinguish small fires simply by spitting on them.

Polite society will insist that you use something other than the carpet as a spit depository, and a lot of chewers find themselves carrying cups or beer bottles wherever they go. This is a self-solving problem, however, since the longer you chew, the less you will find polite society associating with you.

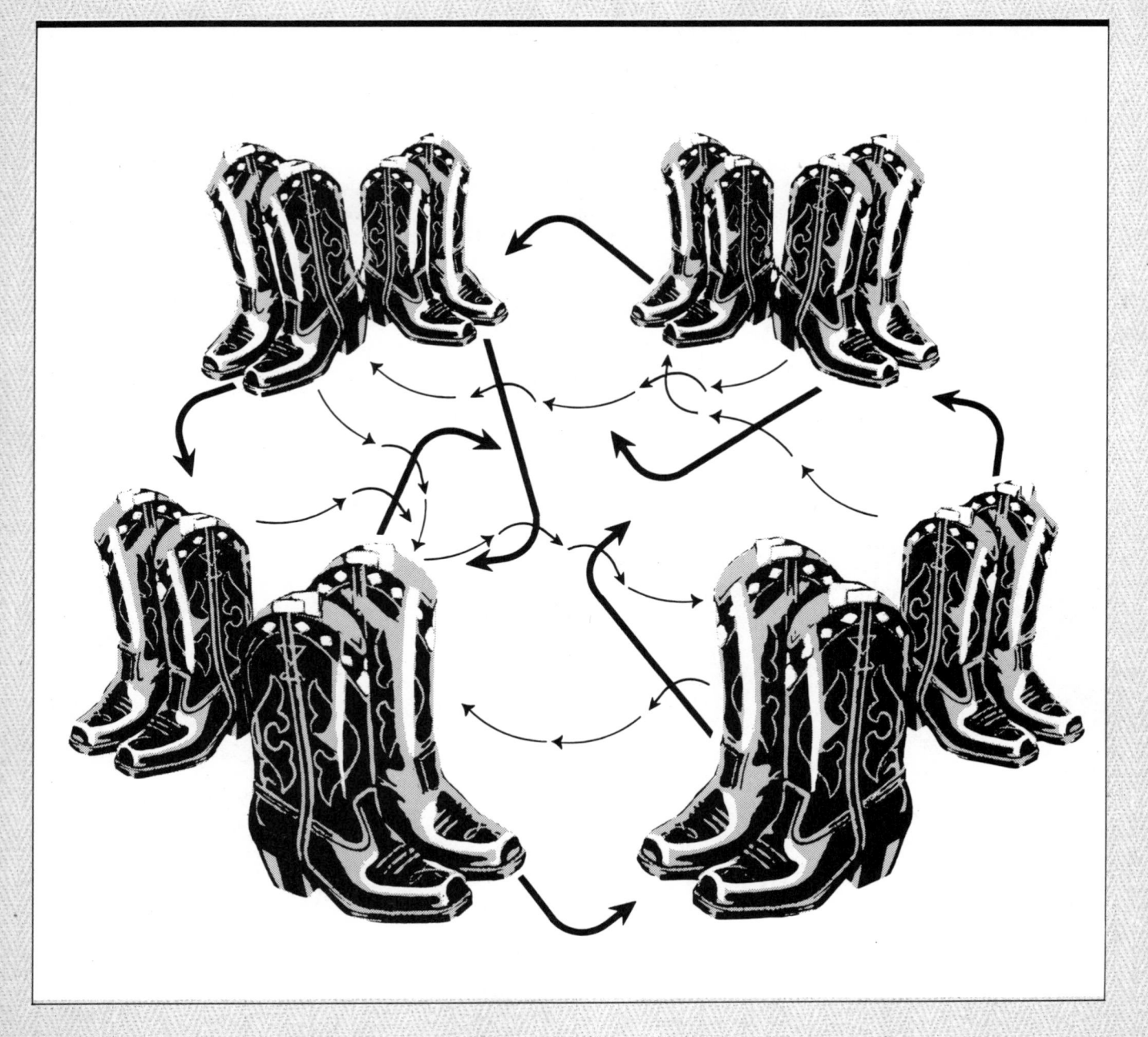

SQUARE DANCING

Square dancing has played a large role in the history of the South. People meet their first loves at a square dance, get married at a square dance, and some finally get killed at a square dance. It's a great thing. Although wanting to go to a square dance can't replace the urge to go bowling, the two pastimes are, in fact, similar in many ways: Both have uniforms, both have teams, both have contests. However, in square dancing you get to hug pretty women. Bowling has never caught on in the South.

The first thing you need to know about square dancing is that it's not a casual undertaking. Sure, you can sort of fake it for a few seconds, but one clod can cause a pile-up, and most serious square dancers would rather have the beginner watch and ponder before plunging into the middle of things.

Southern children have some idea of how to square dance from school, where in many states square dancing is taught as a part of gym class (like soccer or wrestling). Adults who are desperate to know how to dance will have to stoop to the embarrassing depths of taking lessons, or else simply watch and take detailed notes. Actually, if you really want to learn, you will find square dancers very friendly people who are more than willing to help.

Once you have mastered the steps, you still need to look the part. It helps if you have the craggy, furrowed face of a hillbilly farmer, but you can get by without it if you're dressed right. You and your partner should definitely put some effort into matching your outfits. That way everyone will know that you're together and you won't have to fight for your date during the evening. Next, you need to come to grips with dampness. Square dancing is strenuous business. Part of your outfit should be a color coordinated towel that is worn quarterback-style, tucked into the front of your pants. You will find yourself using this towel more than you might at first imagine. Square dancing all night is roughly equivalent to playing two entire games of professional basketball, so plan on using some turbocharged deodorant, and don't wear any clothing that isn't color-fast. (Note: Women don't have to worry about all this, since they never sweat. At least proper *ladies* don't.)

If you are dressed properly, and have a little knowledge of the steps, the only thing that can go wrong entails dealing with the caller. He's the guy who usually stands at the front with the band and calls out the steps. The trick is to understand what the caller is saying. Many callers are lonely, twisted old men whose only joy is to do unintelligible, sadistic square dance calls. A caller will consider himself a success if not a single couple is left dancing or, even better, standing. Dancers, on the other hand, consider themselves winners if they can dance every call and finish in time with the music.

There are about a hundred separate steps that you should learn if you are planning on some serious rugcutting. Here's one of the simpler ones, to get you started.

FISHING

Fishing can be one of the more rewarding ways of passing time in the South, where, especially in the summertime, the living is easy. However, Southerners take their fishing very seriously, and don't expect to experience anything less than a sixteen-hour saga if you agree to go along with some; this can easily be extended to a week or two if the fish are biting.

The first thing you need for serious fishing is a good supply of beer. Three to ten cases per man will usually do it. This provides a sporting handicap for the fish. Next, forget any fishing devices such as flies, waders, or other gimmicks foisted off on us by the British. Southerners fish from boats. How else can you be expected to carry more than two thousand lures, five poles and reels, and the assorted paraphernalia required without boats or bearers? No scenic wading down streams in the South. Rather, view fishing as Southerners do: Aquatic Warfare. Once you've had your quota of beer, anything goes. Sonar, dynamite, rifles, nets, electricity. Also, it's not a bad idea to bring a medium-caliber pistol with you; you never know what's going to crawl in the boat with you. Here are some of the fish you might expect to catch:

Bass. Far and away the most popular quarry for the Southerner. These mommas defy all but the most sustained efforts of capture. It's a widely acknowledged fact that it takes more than $15,000 worth of equipment to catch one bass. Southerners also view bass fishing as a competitive sport, each boat against all others. The camaraderie of bass sportsmen ends at the dock.

Monster Catfish. Very good for those with a large family to feed. There are catfish all over the South, but anything smaller than twenty pounds is hardly worth cleaning. True monster catfish are caught in the deep channels of large lakes. Needless to say, use heavy equipment: 150-pound test line, good hooks, and so forth if you expect to land one of these behemoths. White bread mashed up with liver usually appeals to the monster cat.

Once you have one of the brutes on the line, the tough job of landing it still remains. The only way to get the thing in your boat is to wrestle and manhandle it to the side of the boat, then roll it in, taking care not to let it score your arms with the devilishly sharp spines along its top and sides (a rap or two on the head with a crowbar will temporarily stun the fish and make this maneuver somewhat easier). Experienced monster-cat aficionados will wear some sort of protective clothing to avoid being severely whisker-lashed when the fish regains consciousness and finds itself in a boat.

Gar. Gar are hideous-looking fish, four to eight feet in length and covered with armorlike scales—your basic prehistoric look. In still waters, gar will come to the surface beside the boat and roll slowly over while gliding by. If you can ever get the suckers scaled, they taste good, so here's what you need to land one: a long piece of large rope, frayed at one end, a gaff, and a very heavy blunt instrument. Dangle the rope in the water and the gar (if curious and hungry) will get the rope caught up in its very fine teeth while nibbling. Next, drag the gar to the surface, gaff it well, and bash its head in. Nature anticipated this move and armored the creature well, so don't spare the elbow grease.

Bank Fishing. If you're not into a tax bracket that will let you get out there with the monster killers, happily there's an answer: bank fishing with a cane pole. The enjoyment can be increased twentyfold if you manufacture your own pole. There is something deeply satisfying about spending less than a buck on the entire tackle and pole operation, especially if you have kids. The trick to catching the big one is finding a really tall stand of cane or bamboo to select your pole from. This done, simply hack the pole down, trim all the leaves off with a pocket knife, attach a piece of monofilament line about equal in length to your pole, add a hook and a float, and let 'er go. The only thing left to do now is murder an innocent worm and wait for supper to bite.

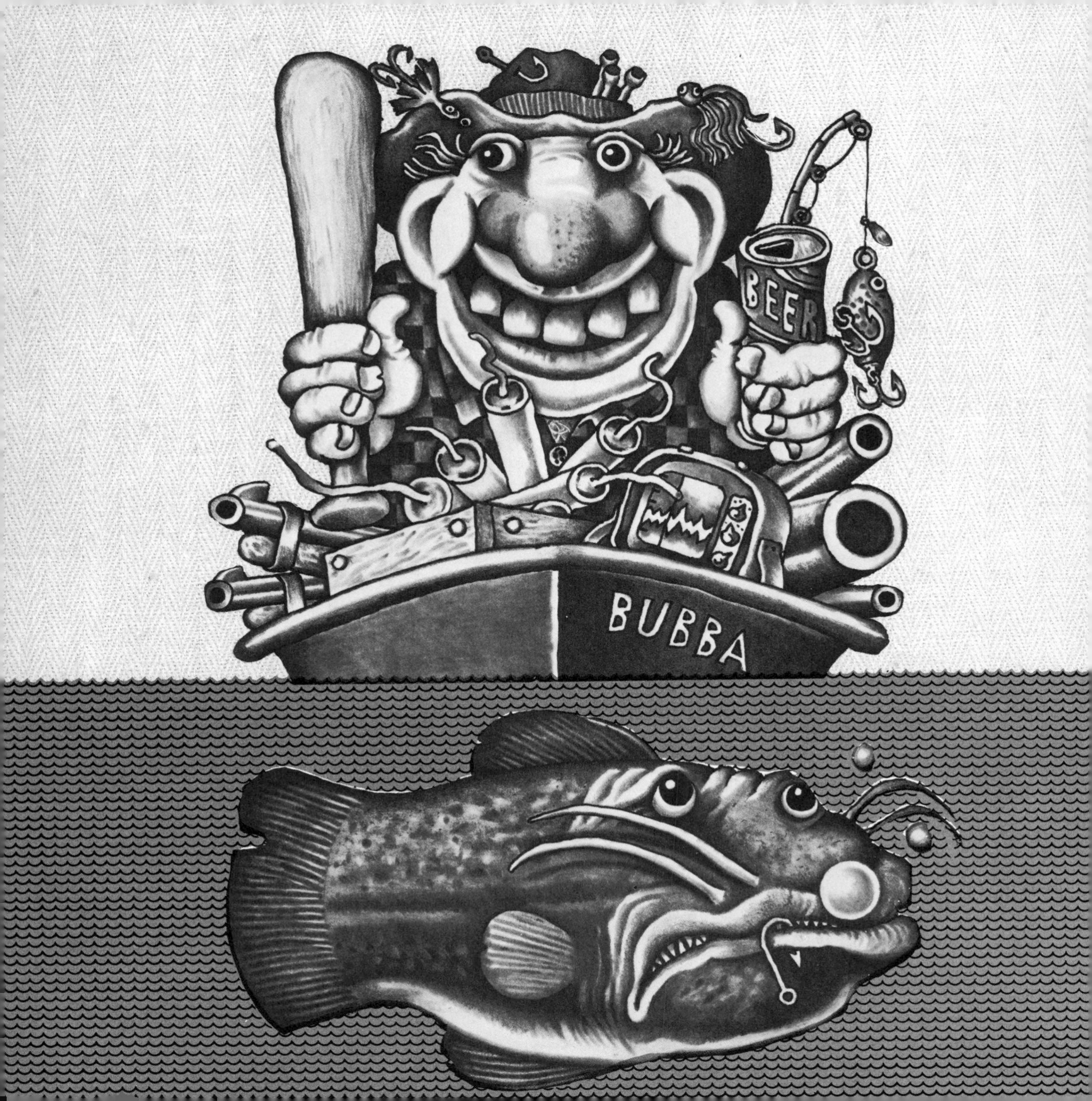

RICH WHITE TRASH

1. Hire Servants Who Look and Dress Like Peers. This creates the illusion that people love to wait on you and inspires others to do the same. It also makes you look like a nice person.

2. Hire Someone to Exercise for You. This will eliminate the unpleasant task altogether, and you can watch as your exerciser grows healthy. After a particularly abusive week of partying, have this person run a few extra laps. You will be surprised how much better this makes you feel.

3. Back Speculative Investments. Show business is always a good one, as is breeding pigs or developing artificial-insemination banks. This last field will supply you with a weird network of business partners.

4. Pick a Home Town. A very small one is preferable; the locals won't give you away when the money starts flowing. Always subscribe to the local paper, and have it sent to all your offices. Maintain an office in your "home town" and never forget to back both candidates for sheriff in any election. It also doesn't hurt to donate a prize for the annual bingo tournament.

5. Make Friends in Low Places. This will give you the air of a good ol' boy and let the public know that you haven't lost the common touch. Bring someone you've met, a local mechanic, say, to all your financial meetings. Let him make a few decisions. This will confuse the attorneys and keep everyone on his toes.

6. Attend Livestock Auctions. Especially the formal ones. These are considered the primary social functions of the upper class in the South. Don't forget to buy something.

Rich White Trash have a strong dose of sporting blood, too. Nothing like a little competition to bring out the best and worst in folks, and it's a great way to vent a few pent-up hostilities. Of course, RWT don't want to have to mix with the scum any more than necessary, and this has caused the creation of many little-known sporting events that have an avid, if diminutive, following in the South. Some of the more popular:

Folding Chair Sling. This popular event has become a fixture at many gatherings, most notably the Poco Bueno Fishing Tournament in Texas. The central idea is to see how far each participant can throw a metal folding chair.

Butterball Bowling. Pins are set up on almost any surface that is flat and has good visibility. Frozen turkeys are then "bowled" from Cessnas or other small aircraft during low swoops. The size of the turkeys and how frozen they remain are left to the discretion of the contestants.

Cross-Country Croquet. Less equipment, but popular nevertheless. Played like regular croquet but with a chosen destination. This is definitely a black-tie event, with the host providing snacks at the rest stations along the way. There are few rules and one would be wise to guard his balls. Actually, this is a good rule to observe when playing any games with the rich, especially in the South.

The North has always had a wealthy class. Following the Civil War, though, most of the Southern upper class was dispersed and its fortunes decimated. Consequently, there is no clear tradition of proper wealthy behavior, since Southern folks were too busy reassembling and reinvesting fortunes during the decades that followed to pay much attention to etiquette.

Now those fortunes have matured as the Sunbelt economy has boomed, and once again the South has a wealthy class. The main difference between the rich in the South and in the North is that here, there is a tradition of visible spending. Excess is the byword of Rich White Trash (RWT); conveniently, the poorer classes will only put up with the ultra-wealthy if the dough gets spread around a bit. Since one out of every ten newcomers to the South will become rich in the first five years here, many will need directions on how to spend those millions in the RWT style. Here are a few pointers that will let you blend in quickly once you become incredibly wealthy:

ICEHOUSES

These abound in the South and are the outdoor equivalent of neighborhood bars in some states. Icehouses call for good conversation, maintaining your balance in the chair as you drink, four or five bags of potato chips, some pigs' feet, a working bathroom, three picnic tables, four chairs, and fifty thousand gallons of beer.

The old icehouse used to be just that: an ice house. People would congregate after work in the summer to get cool by sitting near the ice, drinking beer. Air conditioning and refrigerators put a serious dent in the ice industry, of course, but the icehouse lived on.

The ice business has had a shot in the arm recently with the spread of swimming pools in the South: about five hundred pounds of ice is the only thing that will lower a pool's water temperature noticeably, and the future looks bright for those icehouses that held out during the bleak years. In fact, business may get so good that it will ultimately interfere with the beer drinking, but let's hope not.

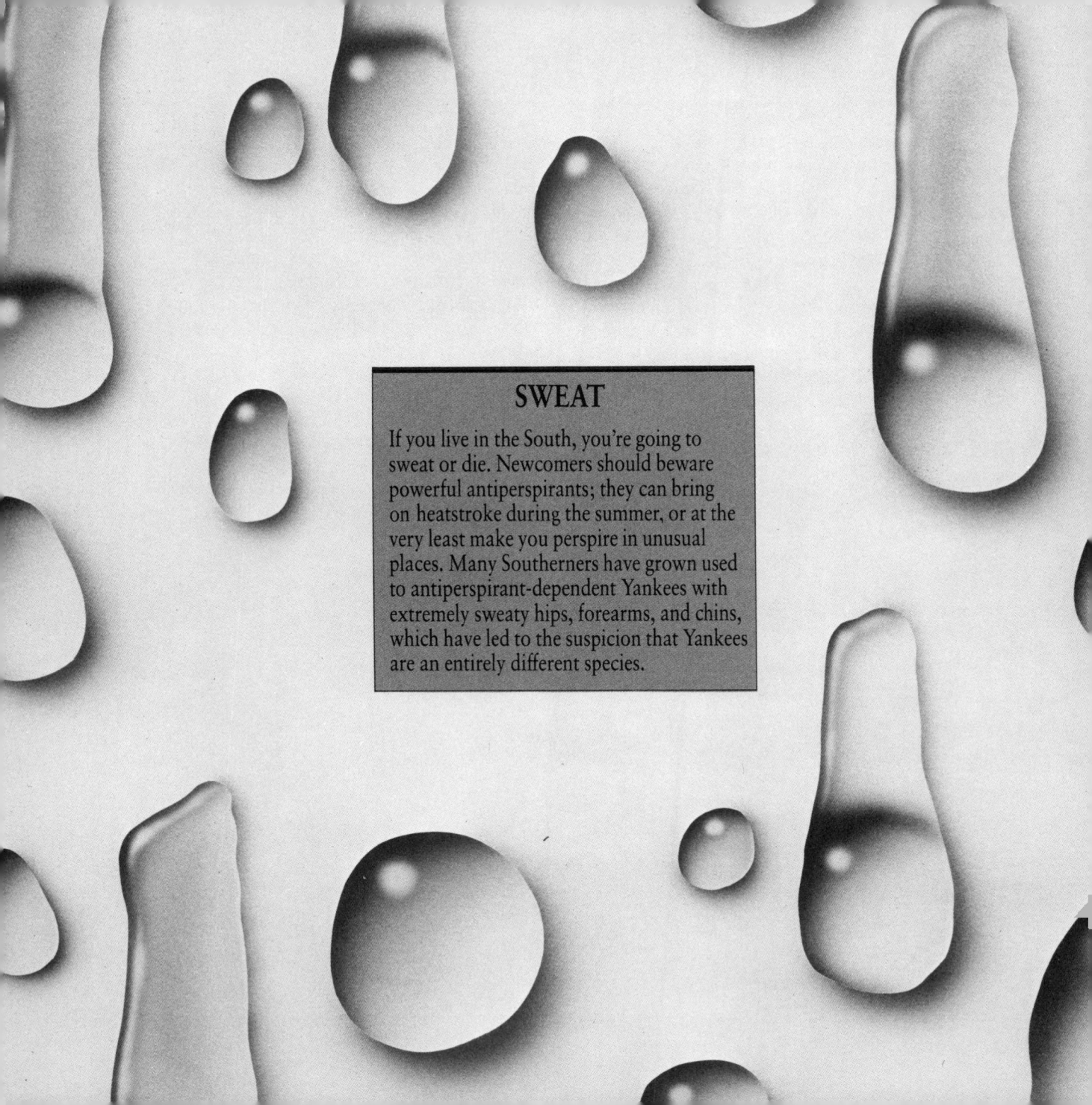

SWEAT

If you live in the South, you're going to
sweat or die. Newcomers should beware
powerful antiperspirants; they can bring
on heatstroke during the summer, or at the
very least make you perspire in unusual
places. Many Southerners have grown used
to antiperspirant-dependent Yankees with
extremely sweaty hips, forearms, and chins,
which have led to the suspicion that Yankees
are an entirely different species.

PICKUPS

There are a number of people who keep their trucks in pristine condition, but this violates the basic idea of a pickup: Dents are a sign of use and add character. Many Southerners will go ahead and intentionally put the first dent in the truck the day they buy it.

The typical Southern pickup is big. No compacts here, please. We're talking about the king-size, extra-long-bed American variety with an engine big enough to pull a battleship. Trick paint jobs and the like are generally considered useless to those who actually use the truck, and four-wheel drive is only going to get you a big round of guffaws from rural drivers who know that once you're stuck in the mud, it simply means that twice as many wheels get immobilized. Winches,

roll bars, driving lights, and bucket seats are other things that you will seldom find on a working truck. But one of the few things that Southerners *do* value in the way of options is extra-heavy-duty bumpers. Pickups are generally driven *through* things, not around them, and a little extra steel makes for less repairs and a more certain future for the driver. It takes Yankees some time to adapt to this philosophy of driving, and often they will overlook the virtues of ram-style motoring and order their trucks with regular bumpers. Detroit has also sold the typical Northerner on the idea of maintaining an automobile or truck with care. This, again, is in direct opposition to the Southern philosophy; if your truck can't make it on its own, then most Southerners believe it should be abandoned or used for a planter.

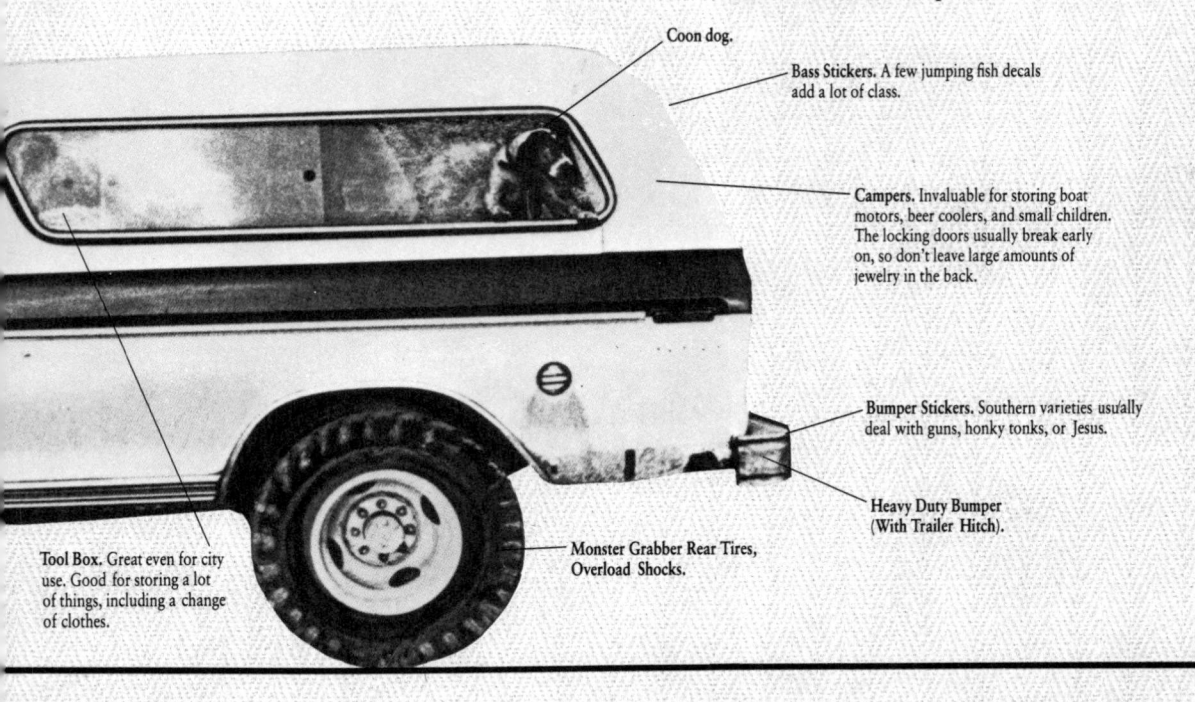

Coon dog.

Bass Stickers. A few jumping fish decals add a lot of class.

Campers. Invaluable for storing boat motors, beer coolers, and small children. The locking doors usually break early on, so don't leave large amounts of jewelry in the back.

Bumper Stickers. Southern varieties usually deal with guns, honky tonks, or Jesus.

Heavy Duty Bumper (With Trailer Hitch).

Tool Box. Great even for city use. Good for storing a lot of things, including a change of clothes.

Monster Grabber Rear Tires, Overload Shocks.

The primary Southern vehicle. There are many other types of transportation in the world, but few are so perfectly suited to the Southern life style. Pickups allow you to carry the family (kids, dogs, and mother-in-law in the back) anywhere. They also allow you to take a lot of stuff with you. On top of everything else, they are the perfect adult toy.

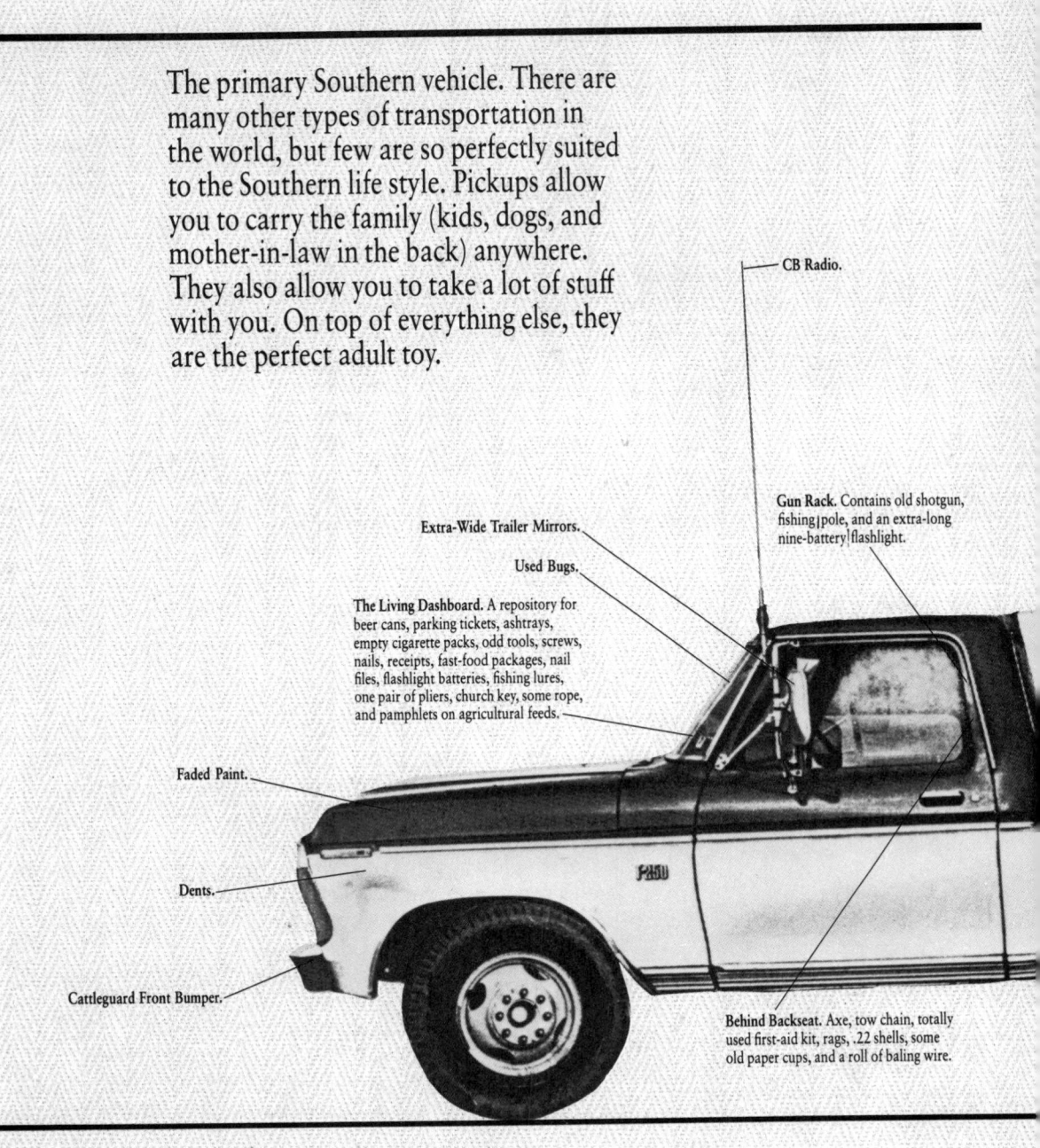

CB Radio.

Gun Rack. Contains old shotgun, fishing pole, and an extra-long nine-battery flashlight.

Extra-Wide Trailer Mirrors.

Used Bugs.

The Living Dashboard. A repository for beer cans, parking tickets, ashtrays, empty cigarette packs, odd tools, screws, nails, receipts, fast-food packages, nail files, flashlight batteries, fishing lures, one pair of pliers, church key, some rope, and pamphlets on agricultural feeds.

Faded Paint.

Dents.

Cattleguard Front Bumper.

Behind Backseat. Axe, tow chain, totally used first-aid kit, rags, .22 shells, some old paper cups, and a roll of baling wire.

DRINKING

being paid on time and will often ask for them before you drink. After you pay your dues, you will be able to get a drink *absolutely free.* Imagine that! If you pay some more dues to the treasurer, he will give you another *absolutely free* drink. If you run out of dues money, or act in a manner unbecoming a club member, the sergeant-at-arms will throw you out.

Clubs are a great thing, so much more civilized than sleazy bars. They also keep alcohol out of the hands of the public.

Sipping Whiskey.
A great many Southerners, especially those in and around Tennessee and Kentucky, believe it to be a major sin to put anything in a glass of whiskey, even a twist of lemon. These are the sippers. They may be heard in the dens and libraries of many residences and occasionally in bars, slurping down some of the best whiskeys they can lay their hands on. The hardcore sippers are not content to use glasses, and instead prefer coffee saucers or salad plates. Pouring a little whiskey into these saucers, the expert sipper quickly swirls the golden liquid while passing the saucer under his nose, then slowly and noisily slurps the liquor from the dish, moaning and gurgling in the process. Like depraved *sommeliers,* many have their saucers tied around their necks so they don't misplace them. This helps, as the sipping often continues long into the night and far beyond the point at which the sipper can still find *anything.* Cognac drinkers from the North can usually make a quick transition to the ranks of sippers, since many possess the same obsessions.

Honky Tonks.
The forefather of the modern singles bar, the honky tonk is where a person goes when he is in sincere need of lots of liquor, a little companionship, and a good beating. It is also a good place to get inspiration for writing a Country Western song. If you don't want to fight, you can always watch other people fight and have a good time anyhow. Patrons go to honky tonks to celebrate or lament the fact that they are footloose and fancy free. This involves cleansing the soul, and that's what honky tonks are good for: the total psychic purge. A good one will take you through the complete gamut of human feelings (love, hate, depression, elation, desperation, contentment, joy, loathing, brotherhood, etc.) and deliver you at the end of the evening drunk, bruised, and with a renewed confidence in life and your place in it.

Picking a good honky tonk is easy. It's important that a honky tonk be small so that you can see everyone and be intimate with the crowd. In fact, "small" is the whole key to a good honky tonk. Most have a small band that will never make it big, a small dance floor (fifteen by fifteen feet), and a small area given over to a few tables and a bar. The music should always be too loud, the women too available, and the bar too crowded. The men's restroom is always out of order, and the door to the women's doesn't close all the way. You get to know people quick in a honky tonk. That's one of the main attractions.

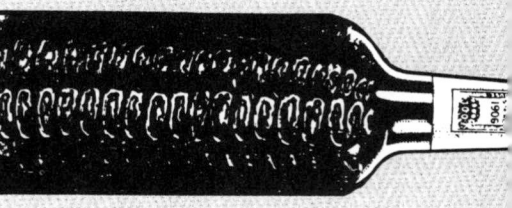

DRINKING

The way felons and woolhats and some of your friends make corn liquor is very smelly and requires a remote location. They start by boiling corn in a fifty-five gallon drum, a process called cooking the mash. After it has cooked down some, they add yeast. This batch is kept on the burner for a week or two until the fermenting stops. The liquid on the top is then siphoned off into a cooking pot (about thirty-gallon capacity) with a sealed lid and a coiled pipe release. Alcohol vapors then leave the pot and cool in the coil, which empties into a collector. It's not the sort of thing that you do when you want a quick drink, but it gets the job done.

Fifty-five gallons of mash will yield about one gallon of corn liquor. Cheap corn and free firewood makes it inexpensive, but there are a number of potential pitfalls (using lead solder in your drums, for one) that will leave drinkers on the floor permanently. Connoisseurs agree that even perfect corn liquor is still a primitive product, and it is judged acceptable if it will make you bite your arm and crawl on all fours. As Southerners still occasionally feel the need to do this, corn liquor can still be found at many social events.

It's wise to remember, before you invite any federal employee over for a snort, that it is highly illegal to manufacture your own hooch. Nothing brings a pall on an otherwise happy occasion quicker than a $10,000 fine or five years in the slammer (except both). Even if you somehow manage to win your case, attorney fees can drive up the price of your whiskey to around $900 a fifth. This takes most of the economy and all of the joy out of the homemade product.

ABC Stores.
It is a widely acknowledged fact that ladies don't buy alcoholic beverages. This makes it tough on a single girl. It's not that she can't drink them, she just can't *buy* them. The easiest way to become widely known as a confirmed slut is to be found buying firewater openly: Any woman who will admit to a lust for liquor is admitting a general lust for life itself, and as everyone knows, only sluts lust. (It almost makes sense when you think of it that way, doesn't it?) At any

rate, the only alternative for the thirsty woman is to shame herself at the liquor store. Liquor store owners, quick to see the problem, even created an alternative: the ABC, or Around Behind the Corner, drive-in store. This allows prominent ladies the option of driving back behind the store and buying nine or ten cases of crème de menthe discreetly out of public view.

Private Clubs.
Northerners will be surprised to find the large number of private clubs in the South; in "dry" areas, there are millions of them. In such localities, it is only within these confines that one can have a drink, so memberships are extremely popular. Here's how you join.

First, it is required that all members be breathing. If you don't breathe, you aren't welcome. Next, you have to go before the screening committee. This usually takes the form of a large bouncer. If you look human and possess no more than two arms, chances are that you will be forwarded to the dues committee. The dues committee will charge you a small fee (usually a buck), and give you a card that says you are a member in good standing. Next you go to the treasurer (the guy behind the bar). He will determine from what you order how much you should contribute as a member in good standing to the club entertainment fund. As these clubs are very democratic, the more a member consumes the more dues he is assessed. The treasurer is a fanatic about dues

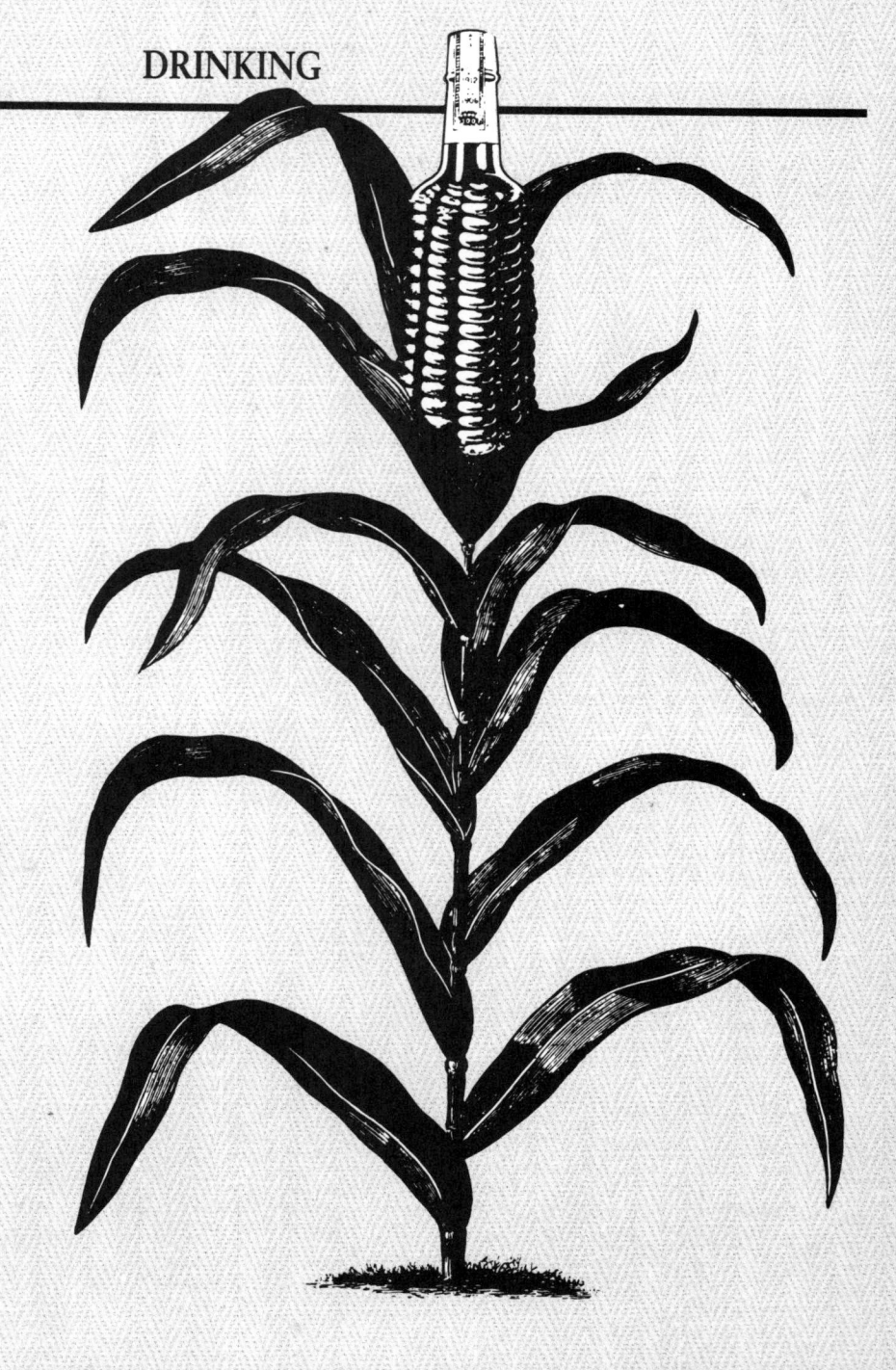

Moonshine. The South has a long, proud tradition of loving the bottle. In fact, only in the South have folks had to resort to producing their own in the years since the end of Prohibition. Part of the reason lies in the ir-refutable fact that the average Southerner has had to endure a lot more suffering than his Northern counterpart. This much sorrow translates into a lot of whiskey, and even at yester-day's prices for bottled booze, few in the South could afford to be sad very long. Thus, moon-shine—handy, economical, and very potent. There are problems, of course. For instance, it's no fun being a hopelessly blind crip-ple, so it's good to know a little about the manufacturing process before you start slopping it all over your Wheaties.

SOUTHERN BELLES

When it comes to ideals, no one can outdo the South. Here, chivalry still lives, and nothing attests to this more than the continuing existence of the authentic Southern belle. There's an old saying to the effect that a Southern belle is born, not made. Few people living outside the South realize how true this is. Centuries of inbreeding among the Southern aristocracy has actually produced women that are physically different from the rest of the species:

1. Southern belles have no sweat glands. In addition to keeping unmentionable stains away, this characteristic also limits their mobility.

2. Southern belles' bodies dehydrate easily, as well, making frequent baths necessary to replenish their water supplies.

3. Southern belles have extremely underdeveloped vocal cords and speak very softly. Many have perished simply because they were unable to summon help.

4. There is virtually no pigment in the skin of a belle. This causes frequent swooning when outdoors, and many complain of fainting and third-degree sunburns.

In spite of it all, belles are loved and cherished in the South and every Southern gentleman worth his salt aspires to own at least one. Prim, proper, personable, pristine, proud, pretty, and pious, the Southern belle is similar to fine art: functionally useless, but beautiful to behold. To offset the burden of their genetic flaws and short attention spans, belles usually come with a sizable dowry and a large family of powerful men who will help any right-thinking gentleman maintain his business, and their offspring, in style. However, before seriously considering ownership, one should be forewarned that the maintenance fees can be grim in the clothing, entertainment, and, especially, mental health departments: Only one in ten belles manages to escape the dreaded plague of chronic cuteness.

5. Being Discovered. This is the fun part. If you have successfully completed the above steps, it's also the easiest part of the whole experience. All you have to do is go to one of the many audition bars in Nashville, all of which are teeming with producers and agents, and wait for the offers to come in. It's wise to spend a few days practicing your signature so that you don't have spasms while signing a multi-million-dollar contract. Also, remember to avoid taking the first offers that come your way. Spend a few extra hours, the whole day if necessary, so that you will be able to choose between the offers.

From here on out you're on your own. You'll have all the lawyers, tax attorneys, agents, and advisors you want to take care of you once you get discovered, and you won't want (sniff) me around anymore I guess, there's not much use for an old dog (sob) and I'll just be movin' along that ol' dusty road (choke) in the rain, where that lonesome whistle blows and the tracks of my mind will wander (sob), but you'll remember me one of these days when you're on top of the world and your fans love you (snort), and know that somewhere where the wind blows free, I'll be waiting to help you when the going gets tough and another drink just won't quench those. . . .

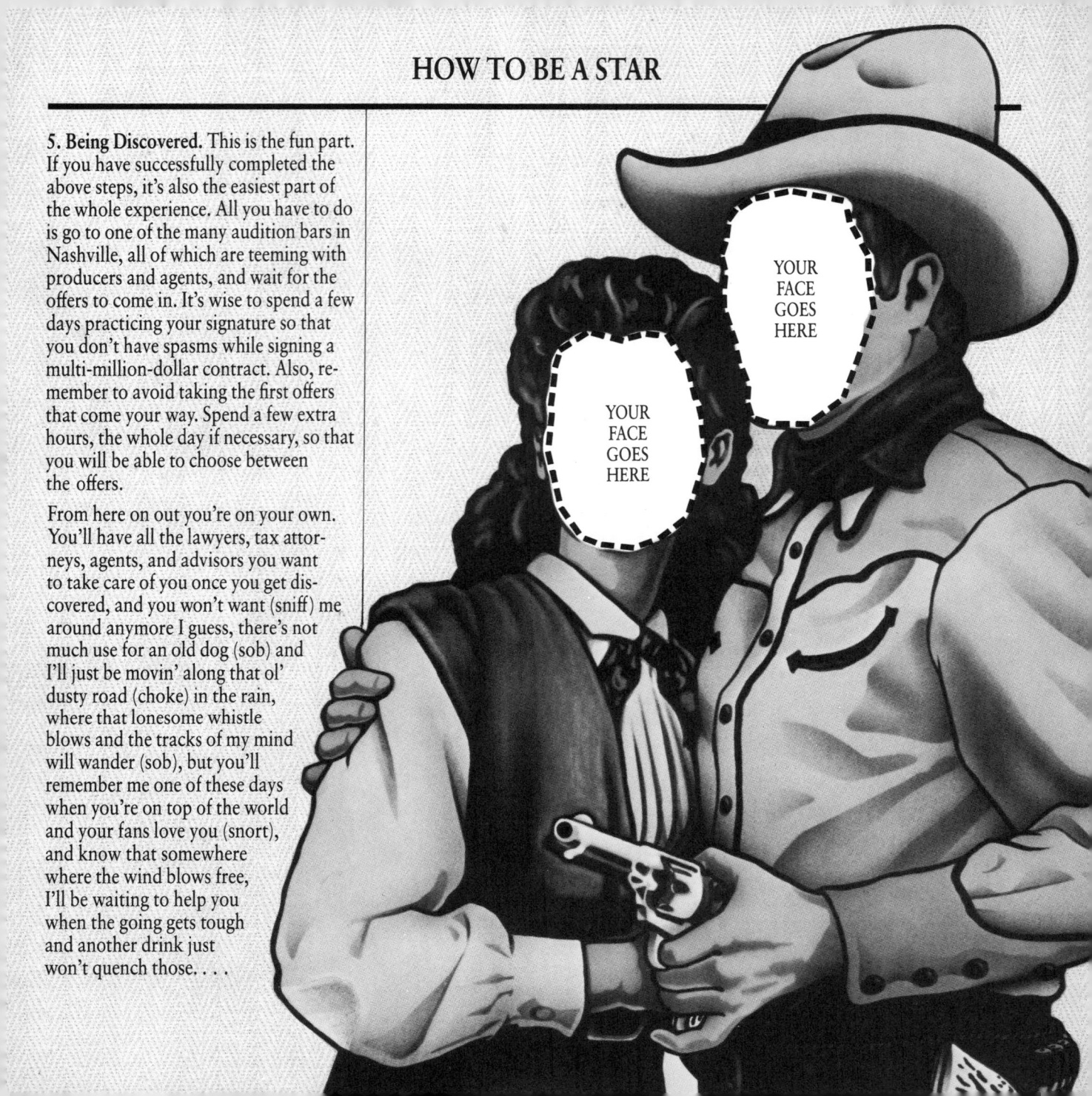

YOUR FACE GOES HERE

YOUR FACE GOES HERE

HOW TO BE A STAR

So you want to be a Country Western singer? Well, it's not so hard if you do everything right the first time. Most people blow it because they don't know what they're doing. Here's a step-by-step guide that will assure your rightful place in the Country Music Hall of Fame in Nashville.

1. The Right Look. This is critical. You will notice that Country Western stars may not always be attractive, but they are certainly authentic. Paul Simon definitely does *not* fit the stereotype. Successful Country Western men have two basic looks: Common and Criminal. The Common Look should come off as earnest, God-fearing, and a little bit hungry. "Humble" is the byword for the Common Look. It's the same sort of look that a small child has when performing his first piano recital for the whole family: self-conscious, but willing to please. It helps if you're a little skinny or a little fat, with a dated hair style like most of the common folks in the audience. With the Common Look, the idea is positive association.

The other popular image is the Criminal Look. This is featured by those guys whose female fans still have their figures. The Criminal Look is brooding, silent, strong. No skinny blond guys here. The body language should say, "Here's my song, and if you don't like it you better act like you do or I'll take your woman and your car." It's almost mandatory to have a prison record, preferably for an avenging murder. This shows character: "They kilt my daddy."

Then there's the most popular look for female singers: The Good Woman. Country Western women are the opposite of Southern belles, and they are far from helpless. The Good Woman should appear competent, wholesome, patient, but have a wild streak that's hidden most of the time. The Good Woman look connotes the singer's ability to bake pies, raise three children, and keep the house clean while working, singing, being a great lover, and saving coupons for the grocery store. The Good Woman is a goal for all lesser women to aspire to. Above all, the Good Woman has monster breasts.

2. The Right Name. The trick for men is to get a name with a literal meaning, preferably related to money. Look at the success of Johnny Cash, Johnny Paycheck, and Buck Owens. If you can't muster that, then go for super-rural names: Leroy, Wayland, Porter, Willie, and the like. This is especially true for women. The names should be Country: Loretta, Tammy, Dolly, Emmy Lou, or anything else besides Angelique.

3. The Right Clothes. This is important. Mainline Country Western attire is usually pictorial, and sequin scenes of almost anything can be added to a bright suit, like maybe a map of downtown Nashville. Band members should wear dark western hats, matching shirts, jeans, boots, string ties, and smiles. The worst mistake you can make is to be upstaged by one of the band.

Another good trick is to dress all in one color, always. Johnny Cash got the best color, black, but there are still a few good colors left. Beware of pink, purple, and other sissy colors as they might not have the effect you desire. Look at Liberace, who simply chose the wrong color scheme and wrecked a very promising career in Country music. Women should wear ruffles, something that would be appropriate for a church picnic.

4. The Right Songs. If you can't write them yourself, at least have the sense to get them done by someone who can. There are about 400,000 songwriters scratching out meager livings in and around Nashville, any one of whom can hammer out a dozen tunes in a flash. The real trick is in the lyrics, and these you should see to yourself. Understand first that Country Western songs are often morality plays set to music; they should have a dose of tragedy. Keep it simple and related to the common man's life ("Open your oven, you're baking my heart"). Here's a list of proven subjects that should get you started: trucks, trains, rain, prison, the road, and, above all, drinking. The only thing you have to be sure of is to *never* make fun of the Lord.

Work Chants. Passed down from the old days, these various chants still work to soothe and pace the modern worker in many fields. Although not widely publicized, they continue in the South, with adaptations to the changing world: "Boss Man says (HO), no time for slumber (HO), give me readout please (HO), in binary numbers (HO)."

MUSIC

The South has a rich and varied musical heritage. In fact, nearly all of the music that can in any way call itself uniquely American emanates from the South. Yankees in the South should be ashamed even to whistle to themselves. With a much larger population, what have the Yankees produced? Nothing. In community centers throughout the South, newcomers from the North are taught the basics of music so they can feel comfortable in their new home. Toe tapping, finger snapping, and humming simple tunes are taught first, with advanced whistling and instrumental courses reserved for the gifted.

You can't be in the South very long before confronting the unique quality of Southern music. It's part of life, and it differs from region to region to reflect the various styles of living and values.

Rock 'n' Roll. That's right. Rock 'n' roll was a Southern invention. Not that this kept the Yankees from jumping on the bandwagon, but they've never really been in the running.

Bluegrass. Hillbilly music at its finest can rival anything going. Considered the purest form of American music by many experts, bluegrass music came right out of the core of the South, and has not changed in three hundred years. In fact, there's only one bluegrass song, played at jamborees all over the South every night of the year.

Soul Music. Sure, the promoters were quick to try and get everyone who had soul to move to Detroit or Chicago, but soul music started here and remains a Southern product.

Dixieland Music. Need we say more? The South even introduced the banjo as an instrument. Where would the modern political convention be without it?

Gospel Singing. Until you've attended a rural gospel church in full heat, you haven't really experienced hedonism in its purest form. What could the devil possibly offer that would compete with the total body-and-mind experience of a gospel choir in overdrive? That's why these churches are among the few in the nation with no attendance problems.

Jazz. Developed by a number of extremely old black men now in their 160s, who continue to play it nightly in the streets of New Orleans.

Country Western. Is Nashville the capital of Country Western music? Can Tammy Wynette sing an ungrammatical sentence?

Zydeco. A unique form of music, incorporating elements of Texas blues and Louisiana Creole music into an entirely distinctive and bizarre sound. It's rare to hear a good zydeco band, but it's world-class dancing music, so keep an ear out for it.

Jugband Music. Great stuff for those who can't afford instruments, this form of back porch music is played throughout the South on any occasion when large numbers of the family gather and are bored.

JUNETEENTH

Of all the odd holidays that are celebrated in the South, the most appealing is Juneteenth. It's the day blacks celebrate emancipation with industrial-strength, world-class parties. As no one was quite sure when to celebrate (the 18th or the 20th), it was simply called Juneteenth. Normally occurring on the 19th of June, many celebrations start the day before and provide a great opportunity for a Yankee to sample real soul food at its finest. Also, don't forget to practice up on your dancing. The two-step simply won't cut it here.

BAR TALK

There remain some basic differences in the manner and subject of barroom discussions in the South and in the North. For instance, Yankees have a distinct predilection for speaking directly to you and standing very close. Some would say *too* close—in many instances, in fact, right in your face. To make matters worse, many will put their hand on your shoulder, or emphasize a point by touching you. This is not wise to do in the South. Southerners have an extremely different view of the proper manner of carrying on friendly conversation. The only time you'll see Southerners speaking in this manner is when a fight is just breaking out.

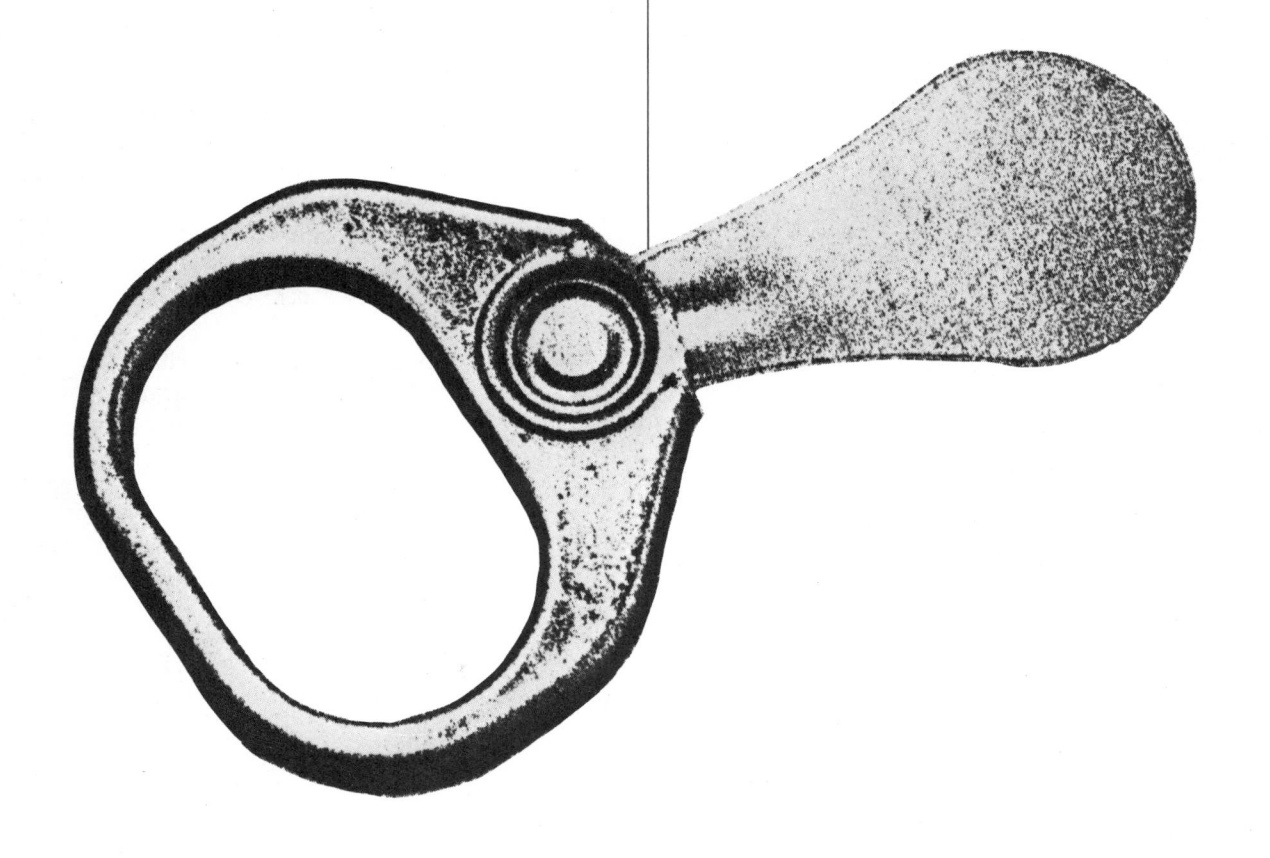

parking lot, in fact, will tell you a lot about any joint. If you can spot an equal number of Mercedes sedans and Ford pickups, you've found a very good place. Too many expensive new cars and the joint is likely to be fake; too many pickups and it's liable to be a dive. Balance is the key word. Beware of new buildings.

Everything in a barbeque joint, including the help, should be old. It simply takes a certain amount of seasoning to get good barbeque, and that goes for the building as well as the food.

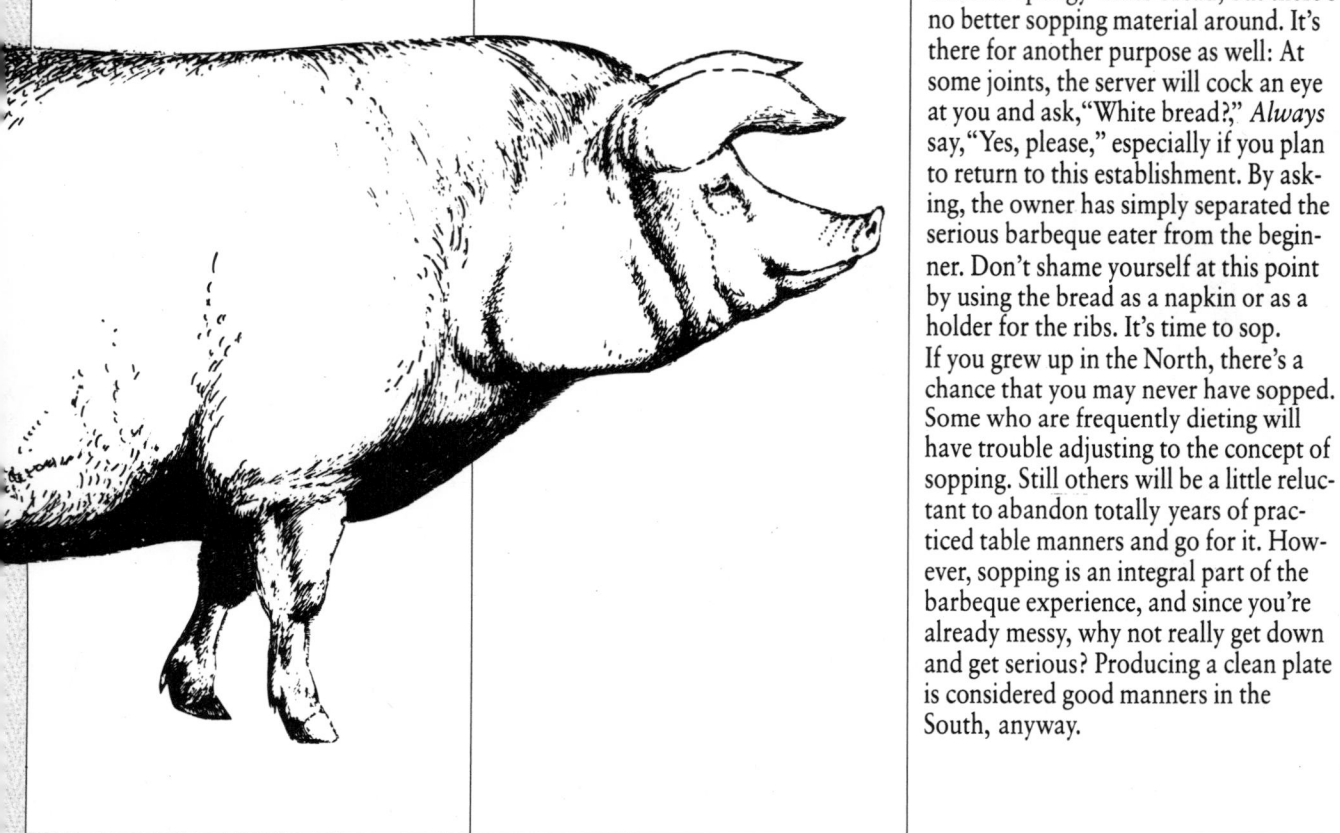

Sopping. At almost any barbeque joint you enter, you will soon come face to face with the only accompaniment considered indispensable by true BBQ connoisseurs: two slices of white bread. No matter how large or small your order, it's always two, never three slices of white bread. Any other bread just won't cut it, and if you see whole wheat you know you are dealing with amateurs. Now, a great many Yankees profess disdain for spongy white bread, but there's no better sopping material around. It's there for another purpose as well: At some joints, the server will cock an eye at you and ask, "White bread?" *Always* say, "Yes, please," especially if you plan to return to this establishment. By asking, the owner has simply separated the serious barbeque eater from the beginner. Don't shame yourself at this point by using the bread as a napkin or as a holder for the ribs. It's time to sop. If you grew up in the North, there's a chance that you may never have sopped. Some who are frequently dieting will have trouble adjusting to the concept of sopping. Still others will be a little reluctant to abandon totally years of practiced table manners and go for it. However, sopping is an integral part of the barbeque experience, and since you're already messy, why not really get down and get serious? Producing a clean plate is considered good manners in the South, anyway.

BBQ

Judging a Joint. The difference between the good, the bad, and the ugly becomes apparent when you are trying to find a good barbeque joint. The first thing to look for is a smokestack. If you can't find one, keep going. Occasionally, you might come across someone who cooks the meat away from the restaurant, but usually this bodes ill. Most of the soul-inspiring barbeque joints are just a little more than an extension of the smoke-box, and should look like it. The better ones usually are about to fall down, have ugly waitresses, and are decorated with everything from motor-oil calendars to old fishing pictures. The best are owner operated, with the whole family involved. The owners frequently look like tractor mechanics: no-nonsense, practical folks who take their cooking seriously and their customers with a grain of salt.

If you find a good BBQ joint in your neighborhood, go there often. Familiar faces get bigger portions. Familiar faces who compliment the food get even bigger ones. By going to the same place for ten years and constantly praising the cook, you have a cheap meal ticket for life.

Barbeque is basically finger food, and in the South, "finger" means anything below the shoulder. Staining your clothes is part of the experience, so don't wear an $800 suit when you are stoking up on ribs.

Unlike other food operations, barbeque joints exist solely because of the reputation of their food. Atmosphere, in the French sense, is not considered important. Other things that are not considered important are complete screen doors, plates, forks, matching furniture, and paved parking lots. The

BBQ

Barbeque is the Great American Food. It's also the most varied, and, fortunately for those of us living here, it's available throughout the South. If you don't like barbeque, don't move to the South; in some sections, you might starve. If you can't find a barbeque joint in the phone book, you're not in the South.

Barbequing has little to do with what's known in the North as a backyard cookout, and nothing whatever to do with hamburgers and hot dogs. Anyone with a match can do that. True Southern barbeque usually means smoking beef or pork for hours, employing secret sauces, unknown varieties of wood, and closely guarded techniques. Barbeque can be a host of things, depending on the area you find yourself in. Although the main rule—the slower it's cooked, the better it's going to taste—always applies, there remains considerable controversy about the stuff.

Outside vs. Inside. Outside or inside refers to what you're going to eat, not where you're going to eat it. The outside meat is usually dry and crispy, while the inside meat is juicier. People have been arguing the merits of each a long time, obviously to no conclusion.

Beef vs. Pork. The most hotly contested of all issues, this one breaks into two camps: Pig people occupy the eastern part of the South, cow cooks the western. You can, usually, get either variety at most points in between. Each cult is a little narrow-minded about the other, while the fair-minded among us agree that if it lives, it can be barbequed. It is possible to find smaller factions championing everything from sea turtles to goats. As always, taste testing is encouraged and the ultimate truth is, happily, still an individual matter.

Wet vs. Dry. This is an important matter, particularly in pig territory. Tennessee has several restaurants that have chosen sides, some wet and some dry. If you are a fastidious person, you would be better in the dry faction since the wet rib eaters usually have things stuck to their forearms, face, and clothing. They do, however, get to savor these morsels for hours afterwards.

Tomato vs. No Tomato. Sauce wars have been a common occurrence in the South since the late 1600s. Almost all sauces have some mixture of pepper, salt, vinegar, water, and sugar. Everyone agrees on that (almost everyone, anyway), but when you get to the tomato the battle begins. Once again, the factions line up vaguely east vs. west, with the west generally favoring the red stuff. In South Carolina there is even a mutant strain of sauce that has mustard in it. The result is a revolting yellow goo that the locals relish, but that will often gag a newcomer.

Surface vs. Subsurface. There is a strange clique of cooks who love cooking in holes. For this fierce and independent breed, you can't have a barbeque without first digging a hole. Pit people have their own methods and rigorously defend deep-dish barbeque as the only road to absolute perfection. Others, the majority, believe a shovel has no place in the kitchen, or near food for that matter. The surface people have thus far dominated barbeque, perhaps because it's easier to move the operation when it's on wheels than to have to keep digging a new oven.

HOW TO STAY ALIVE IN THE SOUTH

- Never swallow your tobacco.
- Never put sugar on your grits in a public place.
- Never take a poodle to a coon hunt.
- Never call a dog a "pet."
- Never travel long distances with more women than men.
- Don't look for the union label.
- Don't use the word "environment" in front of strangers.
- Never say "turnpike" when you mean "interstate."
- Don't miss Christmas dinner with your grandmother.
- Don't wear shorts to any restaurant after midnight.
- Don't stand too close to a Southerner in an elevator.
- Don't stand too close to a Southerner.
- Don't stand too close.
- Back off, Bubba.

JULEPS

When most people think of drinking and the South, they immediately think of Mint Juleps, which is only natural. However, there are hundreds of types of juleps consumed in the South; the mint variety just gets all the publicity.

The Mint Julep, in fact, was invented by disgruntled employees of the Confederate Mint, who took to drinking heavily sugared bourbon in an effort to sweeten their flagging spirits, as they waited in vain for gold shipments from Southern California (South Africa hadn't been invented yet). It soon became obvious, early in 1865, that the Confederacy had waited too long for the gold to be of real use. Thus, about the only things of value left in the South at that dark hour in history were bourbon and sugar, and hence the Mint Julep (so named in honor of its heritage) became a common item of trade for several years following. Southerners who had no money would bet juleps on Derby Day, and soon enough visiting Yankees started adding sprigs of mint to the drinks in a misguided effort at authenticity.

Of course, the Mint Julep is but one of many varieties of juleps available in the South. Here's a recipe for one of the preferred variants:

Meat Julep. Puree a small possum. Take 2 heaping tablespoons of the possum paste and put it in the bottom of a 12 ounce tumbler. Fill the glass with

shaved ice. Add bourbon till the glass is full. Stir and garnish.

Meat Juleps can be made with a host of critters, so experiment, enjoy!

in the road in the North have had dis-
couraging luck trying the same proce-
dure in the South. In fact, one would
have to take a deep, introspective look at
life and its many foibles (as well as making sure your insurance policies are paid
up) before attempting any such action
south of the Mason-Dixon Line.

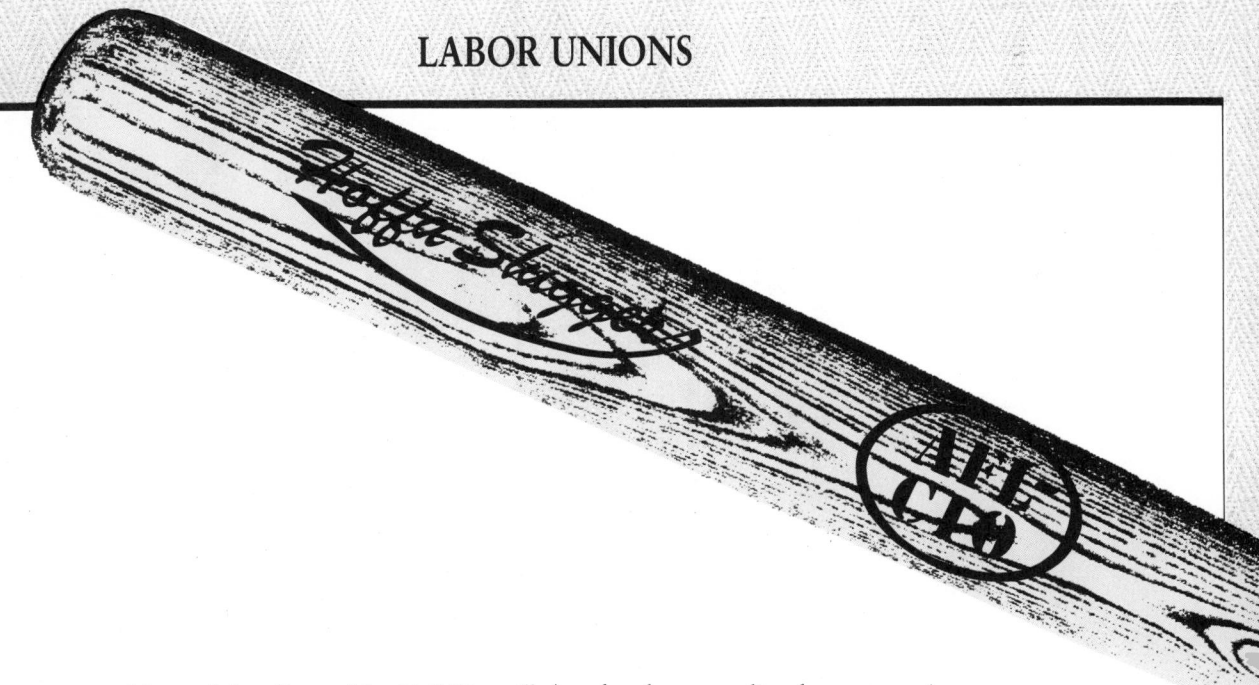

Many of the effects of the Civil War still linger in the South. One of the more notable is a lasting mistrust of labor unions, which started in the North. Additionally, Southerners pride themselves on being independent enough to get along on their own. Of course, many have found it a little tough to battle corporations single-handedly, and as Andrew Mellon once pointed out, machine guns make powerful negotiating tools. The general absence of unions in the South is viewed as fortunate by many, and the excesses of the labor unions and their crippling effect on Northern industry usually provides an occasional yuk or two for most Southerners. And individuals with an interest in Southern history will find that even today they can relive those romantic days before the Civil War by working on a canning line in any of a number of Southern pickle plants.

Thus, new Southerners involved in management should adapt to our native way of dealing with such matters. Always remember to bring three working ballpoint pens and one baseball bat to any labor negotiations you attend. Remember, too, that labor will often have similar tools, but with fewer working pens. "Pounding out the issues" takes on a new meaning in this situation. For those of you who grew up in the North on the labor side of things, be aware that such mainstays as picket lines are pretty futile down here. Several individuals who have stopped trucks by standing

THE BLACK/WHITE TEST

Many Yankees will find themselves confused when they get to the South; the South is far more integrated than most have been led to believe, and it's hard to tell for sure who is who. This is natural. Despite a lot of hollering for the last hundred years, all the races and ethnic groups in the South have been blended to the point that a lot of people find themselves asking, "What am I, anyway?" For these people, we have prepared the foolproof "Black/White Test." It will tell you once and for all whether you are black, white, or something else. Answers are printed upside down and very small to discourage cheating.

1. How do you prefer your chicken?
   a. fried
   b. sautéed in olive oil with a touch of basil
   c. boiled

2. What do you do when someone shouts, "Get down"?
   a. dance
   b. duck
   c. go to the basement

3. The best automobile in the world is a ____
   a. Cadillac
   b. Mercedes
   c. Chrysler K-Car station wagon

4. Colonel Sanders was ____
   a. head of the Kentucky militia
   b. a chicken salesman
   c. an English actor

5. The easiest place to get a job is ____
   a. in a car wash or warehouse
   b. with an international corporation
   c. nowhere; there is no easy place to get a job

6. James Brown is ____
   a. the king of soul
   b. an ex-running back for the Cleveland Browns
   c. a governor of California

7. The term "boy" is used ____
   a. as an exclamation
   b. to summon any black within hearing distance
   c. to describe a male child

8. Polo is ____
   a. a sport
   b. a cologne
   c. the last name of an explorer

TIRE GARDENS

A tire planter is a sign of your total acceptance of the Southern perspective. Here's a chance to exercise your creative juices and green thumb in one fell swoop. First select the proper tire. It should still have some tread on it so that you don't look impoverished. Impress your neighbors and start with a brand new Michelin radial, or maybe a Pirelli P-6. Now paint it white. Other colors just don't look as unnatural as white, and often diminish the contrast between the flowers and the tire. Next, fill the tire with soil. Flower choice is open, but marigolds or petunias are traditional, with petunias the favorite for their straggly appearance. Don't be surprised if the flowers thrive, because tires are great for growing things, as they trap water on their insides. Finally, select the right flamingo sculpture for accent.

GATORS

It's hard to be around the Gulf Coast very long without encountering one of the more than 15 million alligators that live in the swamps and backlands there. While newcomers will often view these playful creatures as a menace, folks in the South have grown to appreciate their quirky personalities, their multifaceted appetites—and their surprising versatility.

Pets. Alligators make splendid pets. They do, however, take a certain amount of getting used to. Gators love to snuggle, and while this is hard on little children, nothing is as rewarding as the smile of a happy, freshly fed gator. While exercising your gator, be cautious, since many Southern cities prohibit unleashed animals.

Guard Gators. It's amazing how few strangers will enter a house protected by guard gators. Although they have the advantage of not barking, the sound of chomping will still awaken all but the deepest of sleepers and alert them that an intruder was in their house.

Feeding an Alligator. This is a touchy process. You must be certain that your alligator can *clearly* distinguish between the food and the hand that feeds. Lack of prudence in feeding these creatures is responsible for the proliferation of Gator-Aids, a prosthesis worn by many Everglades residents.

Gator Hunting. Many people have been misled by recent reports that gators are hunted for their hides and have in fact become an endangered species. This is pure drivel. Ask any experienced gator hunter and he'll tell you that in a natural environment, many alligators simply shed their hide if suddenly frightened. Hence, a veteran will merely sneak up behind a large bull gator and, in one deft move, grab the critter's tail while discharging a gun into the air, causing the gator to jump right out of its skin. There are numerous species of gators highly prized by hunters and stalkers. They include the following varieties:

Attaché—This hide is highly valued due to the handles that protrude from the spine every twenty-four inches.

Oxford—Hunted primarily by shoe and boot manufacturers because of the natural lace holes.

Valise—Another of nature's quirks, this particular species starts its strap when no larger than a man's hand.

Zipper—The backbone of the industry.

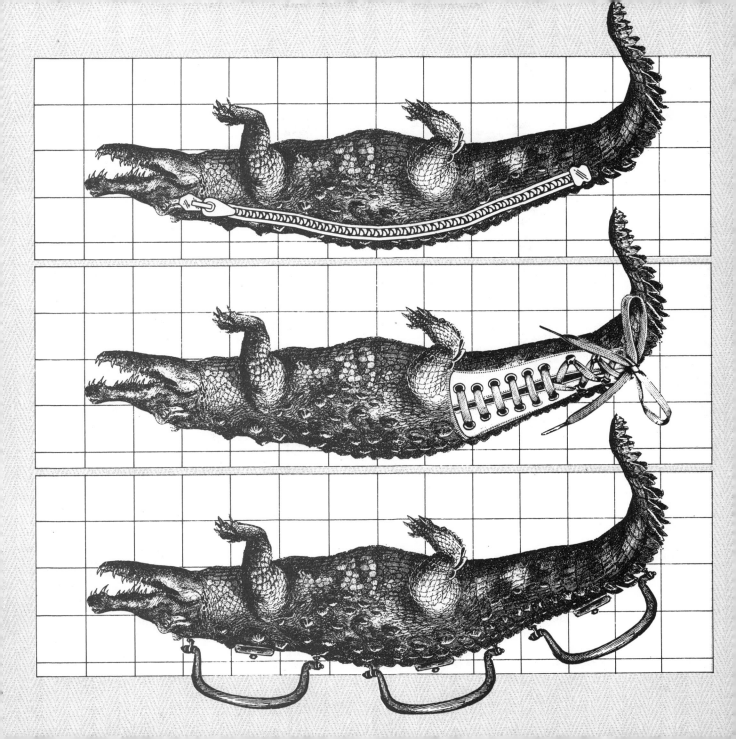

RELIGIOUS CULTS

Holy Rollers. The same folks who brought you the "Frug" and a host of other dances during the early '60s. Theirs is the quintessential release of heavy-duty dancing, joined by the soul satisfaction of a religious doctrine. Veteran Rollers know to ScotchGard their entire wardrobes before attending Sunday morning services.

Ku Klux Klan. California may have an occasional cult or two, but few places in the world can boast of as large or as weird a group as the Ku Klux Klan. These righteous folks, grown men, many of them, dress up in sheets and hoods and then march around burning crosses. That's a pretty heavy act, and we haven't even talked about the murder and torture yet. Compared to the Klan, the Moonies are super-normal, respectable, upstanding citizens. One very good rule for anyone who is not absolutely and clearly white and Christian: Don't go to a linen sale just before a major civil rights demonstration.

RELIGIOUS CULTS

Southern Baptists. This group of worshipers is by far the most prevalent in the South. When trying to make friends with a Baptist, do *not* ask him to dance with you. Dunking a few doughnuts together would make for a better start.

Gospel Church. Sites of the most enjoyable forms of worship, these rural country churches come in a variety of creeds, but share an unrestrained zeal for praising the Lord in song and dance. The closer you get to a city, the better the costuming and choreography. While everyone sings together, individualism is encouraged in dance and gestures, so you better practice musical seizures if you want to mix well.

TV Evangelists. A social force in the South, their influence spreads with every satellite that's launched. It's sort of high-tech fundamentalism with a dash of talk show. The only way to recognize a real TV evangelist is by the aptness of his name, such as Oral Roberts.

Chicken-Fried Steak. These are small steaks fried in the *manner* of chicken, not actually fried *by* chickens. The dish is incomplete without thick cream gravy poured over the breaded steak.

STRANGE FOODS

Blackeyed Peas. A holiday favorite that you will encounter throughout the South at all times of the year. Many uppity, pretentious folks believe that blackeyed peas are good only as food for livestock, but they've probably never been exposed to a correctly prepared mess of peas. They're worse for the bad luck.

Fried Okra. Another Southern favorite, widely known as the "Pod of the Gods."

Crayfish. These redneck lobsters are found all over the Southern coast, but mainly in Louisiana. You break off their little tails and eat them like shrimp. Gourmands and gourmets alike will then pick up the discarded heads and suck the juices and whatever from them, smacking and slurping loudly. Four or more people sucking crayfish heads simultaneously can create a sound that is totally disgusting to all but themselves.

Chitlins. The carnivore's version of chips, chitlins are squares of pig intestine deep fried until they are crispy. They taste better than they sound.

Greens. A wide spectrum of plant tops can be served under this general heading, but the most common are mustard greens boiled and served with peppers in vinegar. Also referred to as "backyard salad."

Steak Fingers. From the deep fryer to you, these are getting harder and harder to find; there are only sixteen fingers to a single cow, and they must be harvested before the calf grows hooves.

Corn Dogs. This is the closest thing to a hot dog you'll find in some areas—a weenie on a stick, dipped in corn batter and deep fried. You are customarily given a little paper cup of mustard in which to dip your corndog. Much tidier to eat than its Northern cousin.

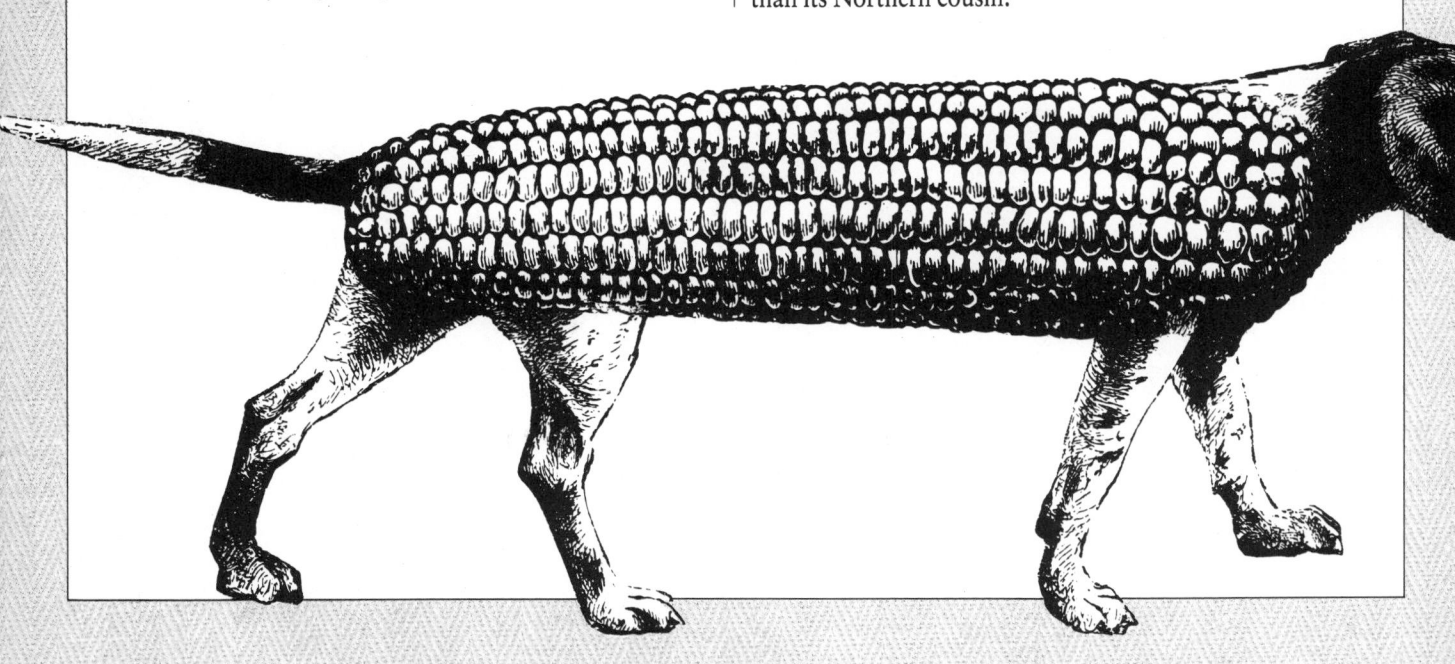

Cornbread and Clabber. Here's one to write home about. This is a favorite of the toothless and the elderly. Just crumble a piece of cornbread into a glass of cold buttermilk and stir. Sort of a hillbilly smoothie. It's a lot like drinking very old cottage cheese, except it tastes worse.

Iced Coffee. This is a favorite in the warmer months. Most use a lot of milk with it. If you have nothing to do for the rest of the week, some white lightning makes a nice addition.

Pickled Pigs' Feet. An all-round favorite, and so appetizing, too. Prepared much like pickled-anything-else, these bright pink fleshy appendages can be found in jars on counters in stores and bars throughout the South ("Don't touch that, Miss Sarah, you don't know where it's been"). Most come from the famous "pickling pigs," which are raised especially for this purpose. The feet are harvested (don't worry, they grow back) each August; this explains why it's very hard to find a tall pig during pickling season anywhere in the South.

Hot Peach Sandwich. Here's one that even the most unimaginative can appreciate. Basically a sliced peach sprinkled with sugar and grilled between two slices of buttered bread. The trick is to mash the sandwich around its edges as it's cooking; some folks use a waffle iron, but a double griddle is perfect.

Brown Betty. A dessert made of apples baked between layers of bread, sugar, cinnamon, and butter. Cherry Betty is another variety; in fact, there are about a hundred different Bettys available, but you won't find them in any but the most homespun cafés.

STRANGE FOODS

In the South, you will come across some very strange things that people eat. Most of these fall into the "acquired taste" category, but the courageous will find themselves developing tastes they might never admit to back North.

DRESSING SOUTHERN

Stompers. There is little in life more gratifying than a good pair of boots. The styles vary depending on what part of the South you are in; cowboy boots are more popular in some parts and Wellingtons in others. Either way, get used to never having to worry about shoelaces again.

The trick to selecting a pair of boots is to go for a durable leather. Stay away from things that are slick or small, like lizards. Instead, go for bull African water buffalo or Brahma hide. Good boots should last for a long time if you don't blow it by getting a sissy leather. Rough-outs (named because the rough side of the leather is outside) are longlasting, but a little too get-down for parlor or business wear. Better to go with something simple and brown. Scuff up your boots a bit before wearing them in public, unless you like someone else scuffing them up for you.

Bib Overalls. Great for an authentic cracker look, bib overalls cover a host of uses and sins. Red Ball makes a spectacular version with many pockets and a flour-sack fit. They are worn without any shirt in extreme heat, and they also double as jumpers in cold weather with a sweater and long johns.

Holster Knives. No man and few women should ever be without a knife. Handy for a host of duties, a good belt knife is essential for the Southern look. Any locking folding knife will do, but be aware that officials at your local airport will take less than a broad view of a large knife being worn on a commercial flight.

DRESSING SOUTHERN

Welder's Hat. Many wonder whether all residents of the South can weld, or if they just wear the hats. Actually, if you wear one of the hats long enough, you do begin to have a desire to weld. Avoid wearing your hat in the bill-forward position. This will mark you as a rank impostor. Welders wear masks; thus, the bill is in the back. This allows the mask to fit into place and your neck to be shielded by the bill from stray sparks. It also means that welders are among the few rednecks in the South who don't have red necks.

Non-Designer Jeans. Southerners spend a lot of their time outside, and jeans are the standard wear for all but the most formal occasions. Only women, however, can get away with designer jeans. People will regard you as a fool for paying more than $20 for a pair of jeans, and nothing will communicate this fact quicker than having some prissy designer's name all over your pockets. If you feel insecure without someone's name on your pockets, then at least have a name that Southerners can relate to. George Wallace jeans, for instance, would be just fine.

Oil Letter Jacket Vests. Here's a hot item. Seems that the glory has gone out of sporting events. Nowadays, the most impressive letter jackets come from the major oil companies. In any Southern airport, you will see young workers from various offshore drilling rigs wearing down-filled vests with platform symbols and lettering. The mortality rate for these workers is appalling, and you had best think twice before making disparaging remarks to anyone wearing a vest with more than two patches. These folks have seen a lot of death.

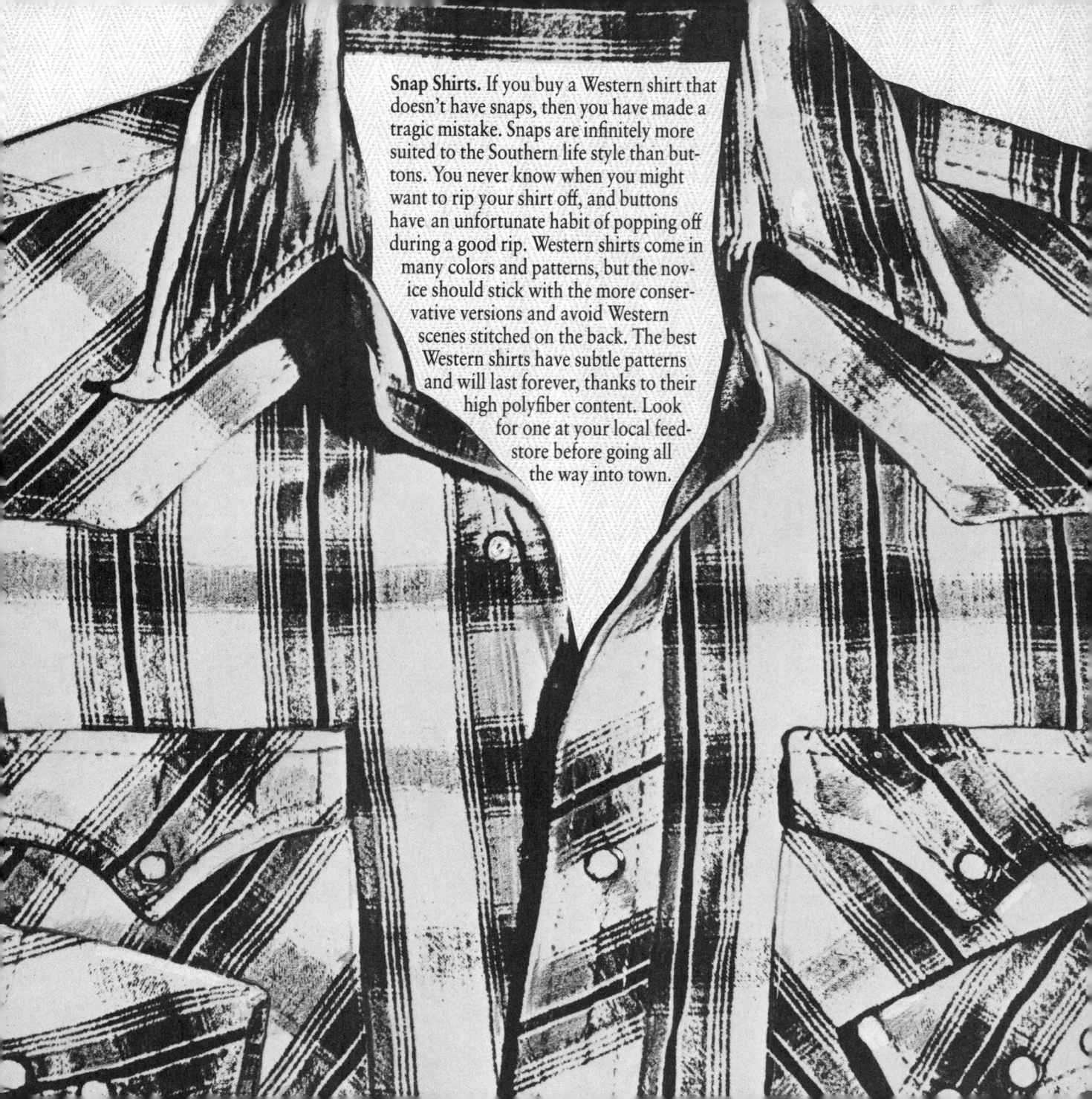

Snap Shirts. If you buy a Western shirt that doesn't have snaps, then you have made a tragic mistake. Snaps are infinitely more suited to the Southern life style than buttons. You never know when you might want to rip your shirt off, and buttons have an unfortunate habit of popping off during a good rip. Western shirts come in many colors and patterns, but the novice should stick with the more conservative versions and avoid Western scenes stitched on the back. The best Western shirts have subtle patterns and will last forever, thanks to their high polyfiber content. Look for one at your local feed-store before going all the way into town.

DRESSING SOUTHERN

Nothing is more conspicuous than an overgarbed Yankee looking for air-conditioning. Many Northerners have ceiling fans installed in their automobiles in a last ditch attempt to avoid having to part with all their wool clothing. Eventually, though, they all come to their senses and start dressing Southern. Here are a few basic clothing tips:

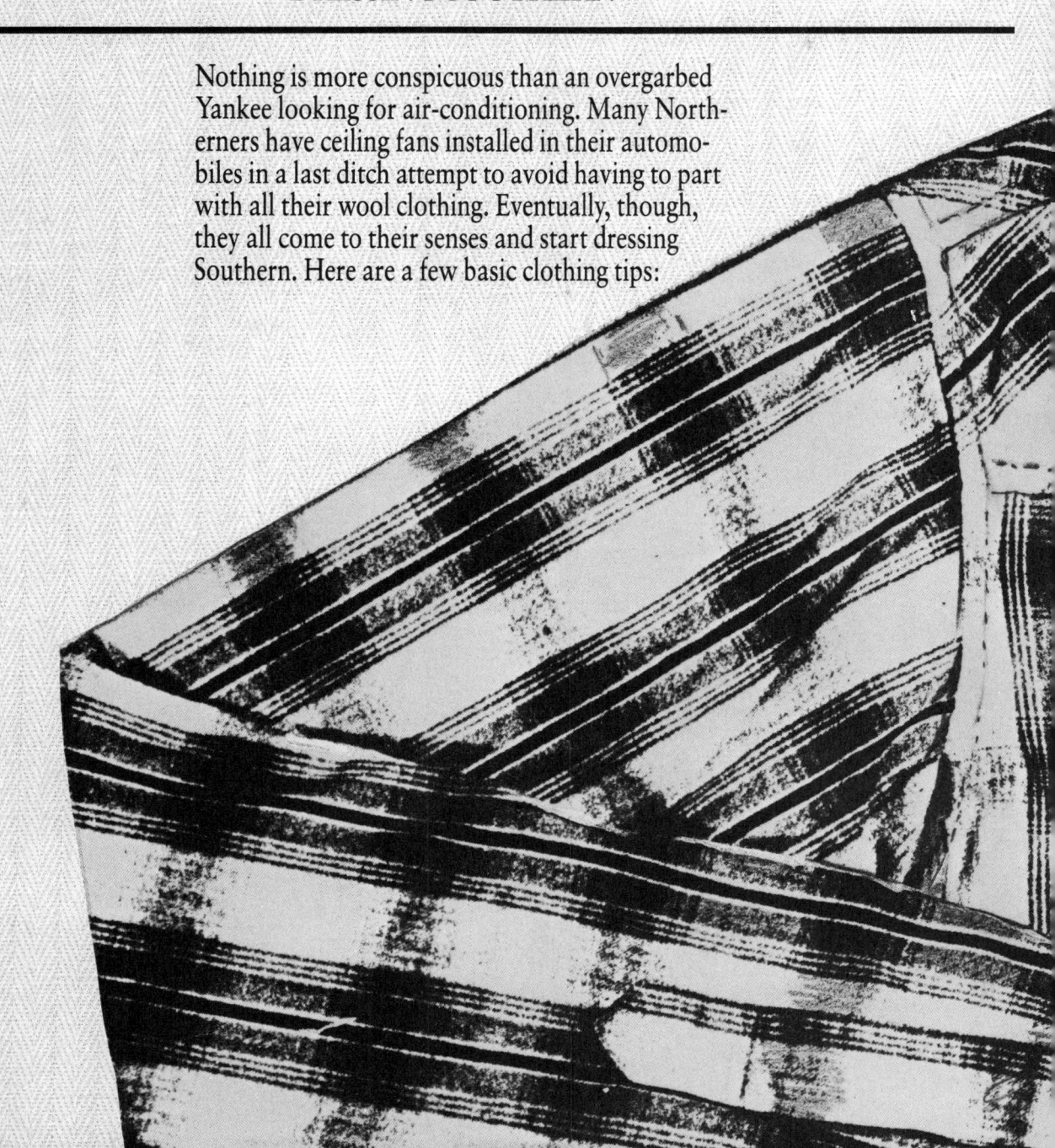

RECYCLING

In the South, there has always been an awareness of the need for recycling industrial products. It was particularly infuriating for Southerners when all of a sudden, about ten years ago, Yankees started talking about recycling as if it were a new idea. We've always found uses for things that Yankees just throw away. For instance:

Clorox Bottles. Who in the world would run a trotline without a Clorox bottle? These are an indispensable part of your fishing equipment. They are used widely as floats for nets or crab pots. And if you cut the bottom out of one you have the best bailer imaginable. Many gardeners in the South also use bottomless Clorox bottles for seedlings, as sort of miniature hothouses. The list goes on and on. If you can't find a use for one, some of your friends will.

Oil Drums. No one throws away an oil drum. They can be made into a host of useful items. Oil drum barbeque pits are deployed by the thousands each year. Slice one vertically down the middle and you've got two watering troughs, slice it the other direction and you've got two planters for the patio. A lot of baths have been taken in drum tubs, and they're also invaluable for moonshine stills.

Pickup Beds. Saw the front half of the pickup off, weld a tongue on, and you've got a great trailer. There are about 100,000 of these trailers used around the South. If the wheels and tires aren't good, then you can keep just the bed, paint it red, fill it with dirt, and plant okra in it.

Beer Cans. These are used extensively in the South to line the bottom of lakes and streams so you can see the fish more easily.

1. Trot Line

2. Funnel

3. Plant House

4. Bailer

CLOROX

BLEACH

CLEANS
DISINFECTS
REMOVES STAINS

BIBLE BELT

Most Yankees have heard about the bible belt, but few have actually ever seen it. Naturally, many have questions about the bible belt: How big is it? What color is it? Well, the real bible belt is in the South. It's black and white and comes in adjustable waist sizes. It's awarded annually to the Southern evangelical preacher who performs the most inspiring miracle in a tent.

The current holder of the Southern Bible Belt is the Reverend Jeremiah Luke Walmsly, a Southern Baptist preacher who, before an audience of more than 80 souls, turned two totally blind men stone deaf. This is the second year the Reverend Luke has worn the belt, having only a year ago turned three cases of wine into water at a Salvation Army kitchen in downtown Mobile, Alabama, bringing tears to the eyes of everyone present.

FLORIDA: SOUTH OF THE BORDER

Boat Races. You have to get up early for the best ones, usually about two hours before sunrise. The standard races occur between Coast Guard cutters or fast-pursuit patrol boats and the home team boys in cigarette racers. The cigarette racers are beautiful, sleek, and expensive sea rockets. The locals have the advantages of speed and the will to win, since heavy-duty prison sentences await should they lose the race.

Learning a Second Language. One of the troublesome aspects of the great influx of Central and South Americans in Florida is the necessity of learning their language. At least seven dialects of Spanish are now spoken in Miami, with more to come. A beginning course in Spanish will stand you in good stead, but here are a few common phrases to get you started on the right foot:

Buenos días, señor.	Good day, Sir.
¿Como está usted, mi amigo?	How are you, my friend?
Zorro Hábil Tres a Jefe Carlito, estamos descubiertos, (nos han descubrido) repite, estamos descubiertos.	Able Fox Three to Charlie Leader, we are discovered, repeat, we are discovered.
Tres cajas de granadas y un proyectil superficie-a-aire, por favor.	Three cases of grenades and a surface-to-air missile, please.
¿Cuantos hombres estarán en el sitio d'aterrizaje?	How many men will be at the landing site?
(Sorbo.) Esto sí es bueno.	(Sniff.) This is really good stuff.
Cualquieras travesuras y te encontrarán en el golfo llevando chanclos de cemento.	Any tricks and they'll find you in the Gulf wearing concrete overshoes.

FLORIDA: SOUTH OF THE BORDER

Florida is no longer part of the South, or even of the United States. What it actually has become is the capital of Latin America. What with one Caribbean coup after another, all the guerilla forces in exile, and the incredibly robust drug traffic, it's getting downright risky to make friends there. The Mafia is active, too, and Dade County is sort of a quasi-DMZ, with one out of every three deaths the result of machine-gun fire. To all of this you add the wonderful climate, resort facilities, and Disney World and you've got great potential for world-class amuck-running.

About the only positive thing you can say about the situation in Florida is that it's lowering the crime rate in the rest of the United States; half of the nation's criminals are being drawn to the alluring opportunities there. In the middle of all this are the oldsters who have plopped down their savings to move to a place with good weather and no crime, there to while away pleasantly their golden years watching the "games" that go on daily. Some of the more popular diversions:

The Beach. As in most of the rest of Latin America, there are wonderful beaches in Florida. Inexplicably, a large number of Floridians seem to be going to the beach at night, presumably to avoid mingling with the tourists. Federal authorities frequently interrupt their enjoyment, and often the spoils of huge smuggling operations come floating to shore over the subsequent few days. This has resulted in a popular grassroots movement arrayed behind the slogan "Save the Bales." Save the Balists have been actively harvesting abandoned bales of marijuana almost as soon as they appear in the surf. This has changed the look of beach fashion and substantially altered what is considered necessary equipment for a day's outing. Black sun screen under the eyes and camouflage swimwear are "in," and few show up on Florida's western beaches without a gaff and some sort of automatic weapon. A Kalashnikov assault rifle is the chic choice.

COCKFIGHTING

First of all, never call a cockfight a chicken fight. Chickens don't fight. They lay eggs.

In the South, cockfighting is sort of the poor man's horse racing. Betting is heavy, and the events are not terribly well attended by those who don't have a passionate interest in such matters. However, nothing is more satisfying than watching your opponent's cock knocked in the dirt with a well-placed hook to the wing.

Fighting cocks are easily recognized by their stainless-steel spurs and cauliflower combs. Southerners have an unyielding belief in the comeback, and consequently most cockfights are to the death unless the trainer throws in either the towel or a large dog to stop the fight. Once you get over the initial bloodletting, you'll find cockfighting to be as civilized as other sports such as bullfighting or hunting eagles from helicopters.

CHIGGERS

Chiggers are part of the Southern experience. They are extremely vile, tiny little bugs that live everywhere, particularly in grassy areas. Or in the woods. Or anywhere else that a person might go.

Chiggers come out in the warm months, get in your skin, and make you itch terribly. A severe case of the chiggers will result in frenzied scratching and temporary loss of all sanity. One of the precautions you can take is to tuck your pants into your socks when you're out walking. This looks pretty weird, but it works.

The little brutes are seemingly impossible to get out of your skin, and countless baths in Epsom salts and baking powder are just a beginning. Washing with Clorox, or covering afflicted areas with Chapstick or nail polish, sometimes works. The only effective way of dealing with chiggers is to let the little devils have their fill and then they will drop off your body on their own. Meanwhile, use a camphor product or lotion to reduce (not even remotely relieve) the itching.

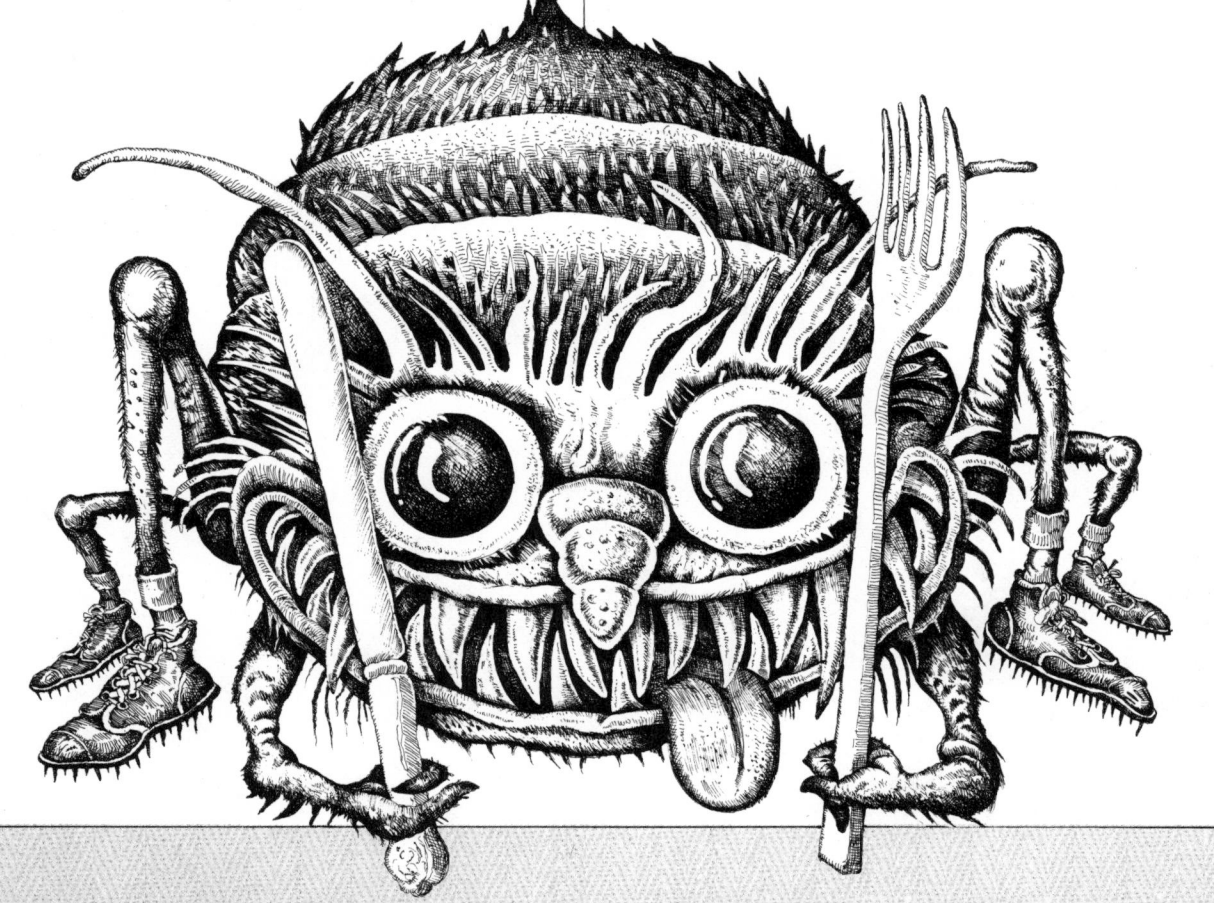

DUELING

Dueling Banjos. Everyone's familiar with this one, right? Well, keep your fingerpicks handy because you never know when that old familiar intro might pop up and you'll be on the spot. It's easy to come out ahead on this one if you simply learn one hard piece, like Bach's *Toccata and Fugue in D Minor.*

Dueling Calves' Livers. Hard to beat for dramatic effect. Each opponent gets a fresh calf's liver. Standing one pace apart and with one hand behind their backs, the opponents slap each other with the warm livers until one man moves his feet, surrenders, or throws up. This is a very bloody event, but relatively painless (except to the calves).

Dueling Chainsaws. A good weapon choice for rural spats. Be cautious who you pull this one on, since a great many Southerners grew up with chainsaws and have more than a novice's abilities with it. You will usually discover that it's hard to find a second when chainsaws are chosen.

Dueling Shotguns and Pickups. The most common of serious dueling weapons. Usually starting in the parking lot of a honky tonk and moving to the highway, the opponents set out to first bash each other with their trucks, then blow each other's windows out with their shotguns. Don't play this one unless you're in a solemn mood and convinced of the righteousness of your position. Occasional casualties.

Fig. 24   Fig. 25   Fig. 26

DUELING

Maybe it's because there just isn't enough crime in the South (except in a few of the larger cities), or maybe it's just tradition, but dueling is still practiced. There are two basic types: dueling for sport and entertainment, and dueling for honor and bloodlust. Sometimes the line is thin.

Since most forms of dueling involve some amount of skill, newcomers should practice a bit on the basics to emerge victorious. A saving grace for the beginner, though, is that the party challenged gets to pick the weapons, and you can usually come up with something with which you are somewhat accomplished. Here are some of the more popular forms:

Fig. 21   Fig. 22   Fig. 23

SPEAKING SOUTHERN

Y'all. King word in the South. Can be used in the singular or the plural, even though it's a plural contraction. Awfully good for addressing groups and getting their attention. "Y'all listen up; supper's on the table."

Yessir and Nosir. Anyone with respect for his elders will use "sir" or "ma'am" when answering any person two or more months his senior.

Yessum. No one knows how this one got started, but for some reason, when replying to a lady in the positive, it's perfectly OK to say "Yessum, I did it this afternoon." This expression probably was started by black slaves as a contraction of "Yes, madam." The reason there is no negative version is that you didn't want to admit to the lady of the house that something was forgotten, not if you were one of 2,000 very expendable slaves. Consequently, it was always "Yessum" whether it was done or not. No point in muddying the waters.

Fittin' and Fixin'. These both mean "about" or "preparing" and are pretty much interchangeable. "I'm fixin' to whup you about the head and shoulders."

Bidness. Means "business," but is the rural version: "I got some bidness to take care of in town."

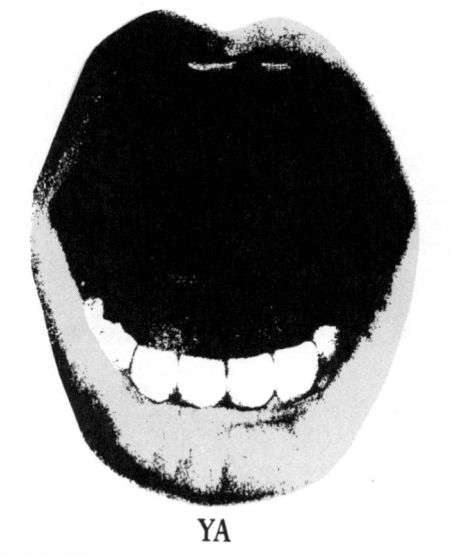

YA

—

ALL

SPEAKING SOUTHERN

There are several basic things the Yankee will notice immediately about the manner in which Southerners speak. First, everything is slowed down by about half. You can practice speaking Southern in advance by putting your finger on a record and listening to Little Richard sing baritone, as if he were drowning in Quaaludes. Although this will give you the cadence, the lilt and meter will have to be picked up firsthand. Here are some guidelines that may prove useful in casual conversation.

Keep Your Distance. Southerners consider it rude to speak into each other's faces. There's all the space in the world in the South, so use it.

Hisself. This is a word in the South and is pronounced IS-SAY-EFF. For instance, "'The water's never gonna clear till you get the hogs outa the creek,' he said to hisself."

Names. Women (or girls) are often addressed as "Miss _____" until they are considered adults. This occurs either after they are married, after they have debuted, or after they have committed a grievous social error. Until such time, however, it's "Well, I declare, Miss Mary, you're all growed up now."

Parents. There are few options here. It's either "Daddy" or "Momma."

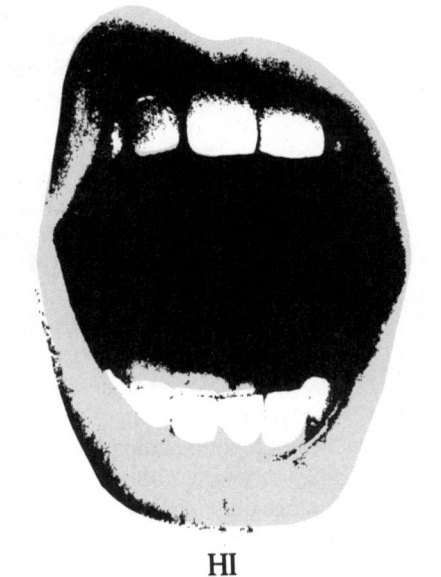

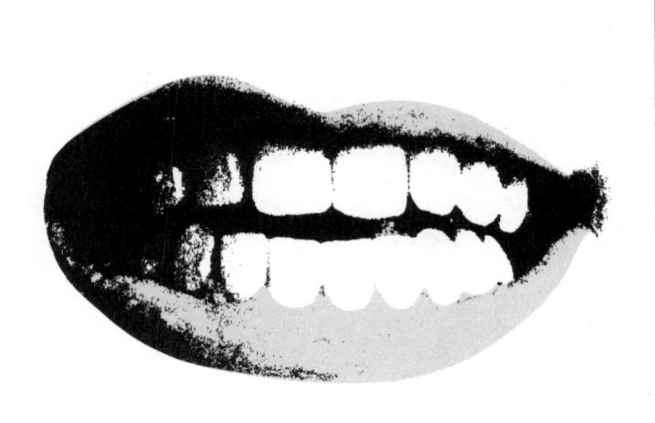

HI — DY

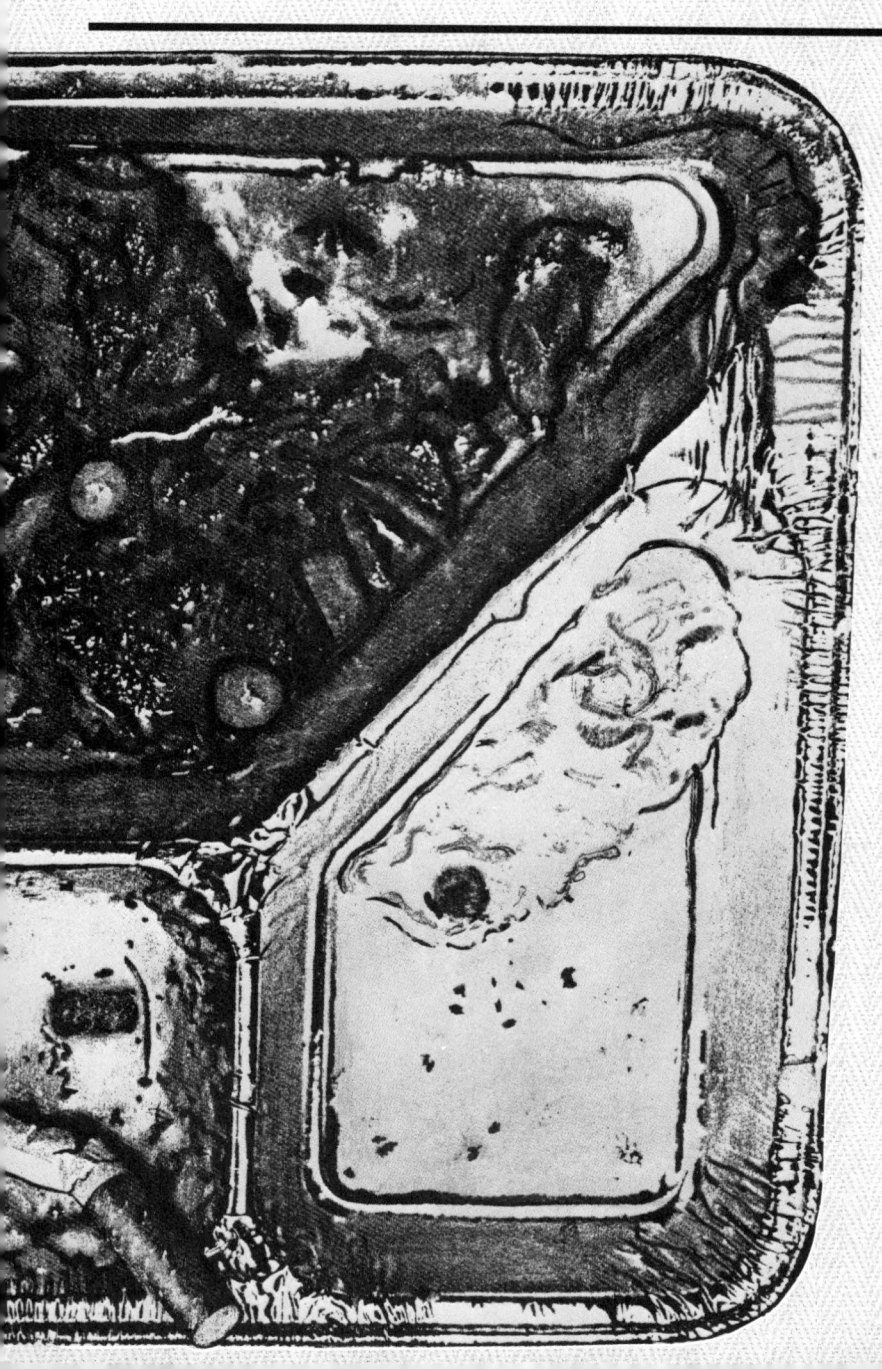

TV dinners are ideal for PWT entertaining, and there are few pastimes more popular than having the neighbors over to watch the wrestling matches while quaffing down a few before the dinners are cooked. The foil dishes also double as ashtrays for after-dinner smoking.

Canned Meats. Many young men from PWT families are amazed at how good the food served in our nation's armed forces is, and most bring back a taste for the countless varieties of canned processed meats that are the mainstay of the service. An all-time PWT favorite is the inimitable Vienna sausage sandwich, or the *Petit Saucisson en Bidon*, as it is known to gourmets around the world. You simply lay four to six of the Viennas (vie-EE-ners) between two pieces of white bread and cover liberally with Miracle Whip and chow-chow. A more formal lunch will call for the popular Spam Kiev, traditionally served with shoestring potatoes.

Formal Dining. Even PWT occasionally have a sit-down family meal, complete with plates and flatware. This usually marks some special holiday or a visit by a wealthy relative. For occasions such as these there is only one dish that will satisfy: Fried Bologna. Each slice is delicately sautéed in bacon grease until it curls into a hemisphere, indicating doneness. Elaborate bologna dinners will include a wedge of lettuce with bright-orange dressing, blackeyed peas, and maybe some mustard greens for color balance. Dessert is optional.

PWT DINING

Poor White Trash helped to pioneer a lot of the food products that today we take for granted. In an early effort to avoid washing dishes, they were the first to try and, later, fully embrace the concept of fast food. There's not a fried-chicken stand in the South that doesn't owe its early existence to PWT. Today, while PWT still frequent the fast-food operations, they usually do so only for weddings and other special occasions. Some of the more outstanding examples of PWT cuisine follow:

TV Dinners. There is not another group in the U.S. that eats as many frozen dinners as PWT. Most people who have only dallied in the TV dinner market probably believe that these things are easily prepared, but there is an art to cooking them. And most PWT husbands would pout for three to four days if they were served one that didn't have the foil peeled back to "crisp" the fries. Also, there are countless ways of augmenting a TV meal with a host of garnishes such as sweet pickles, pigs' feet, or hot pickled okra. The more delicate dishes, such as Salisbury steak, will have the foil-top punctured with a fork several times to allow a limited amount of moisture to escape, thus enabling the glutinous gravy to congeal properly. The list of hints goes on and on, with proper techniques passed on from mother to daughter as cherished secrets.

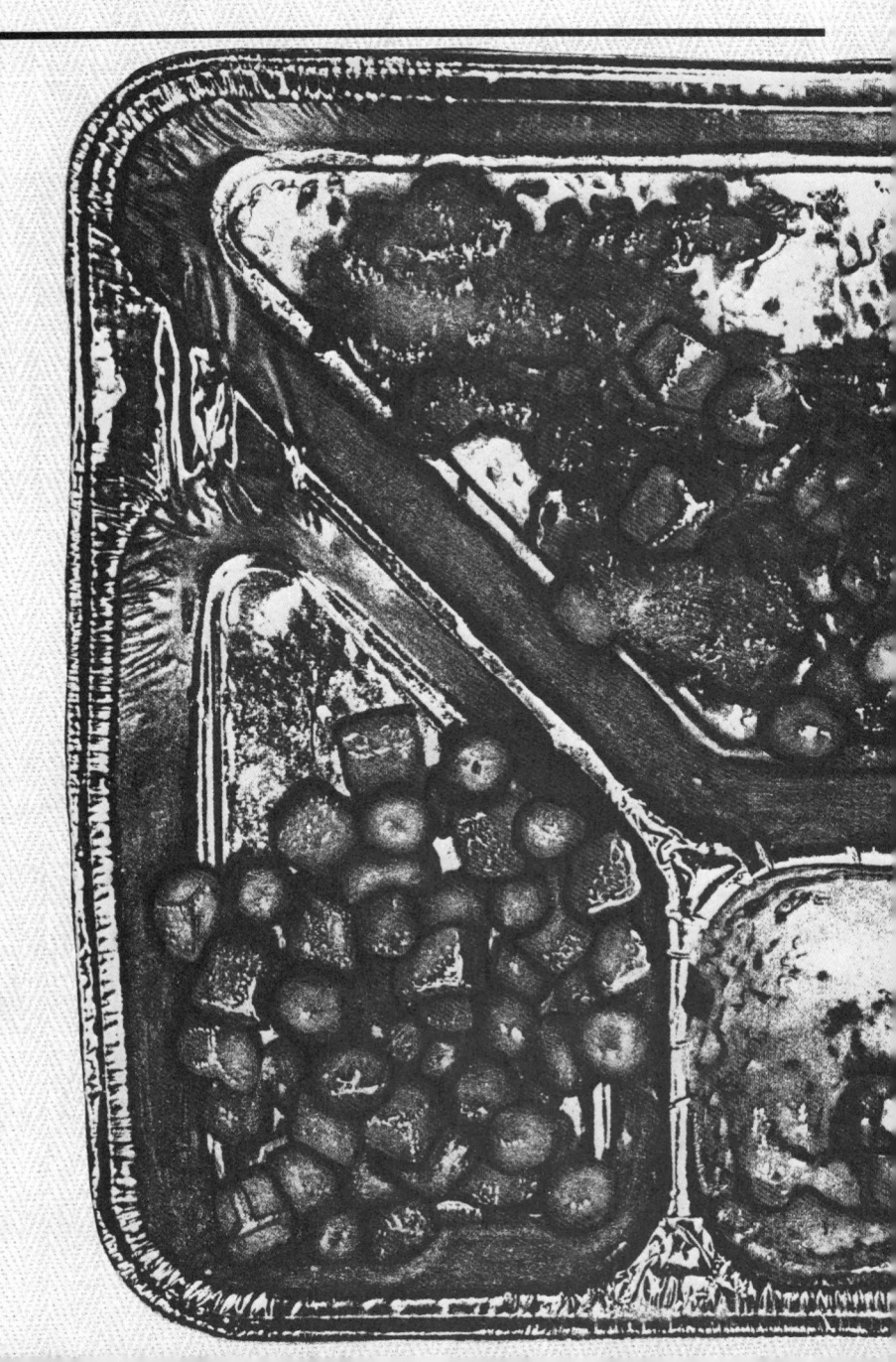

RECOGNIZING PWT

This is getting tougher and tougher, since a lot of affluent Americans have occasionally taken to wearing PWT clothing. However, PWT never stray from the abiding habits of the breed.

The Polyester Patina. PWT are fools for scientific progress. They have few of the old hang-ups about natural materials. Most look for a DuPont logo with the same zest that other Americans seek out the Good Housekeeping seal. They have learned that such items don't wear out as quickly as the natural variety, and also come in day-glow colors so they're easy to locate. In furnishings as well as clothing, an authentic PWT will go for the polymer. PWT were the first to accept, and then to demand, wood-grained vinyl.

The Informal Approach. PWT have broadened the characteristically casual attitude to encompass all of their lives. Dull, repetitive tasks such as making the bed, washing the baby, or emptying the garbage have been eliminated from the PWT life style as time consuming and unnecessary. PWT items are seldom washed and never repaired. Dressing itself is done on a "need only" basis, and it's not unusual for PWT women to spend three or four days in houserobes, curlers, and scuffs until an event mandates more formal attire.

PWT PHILOSOPHY

Not everyone can attain the PWT perspective easily. First, you have to let go of many of your middle-class hang-ups about possessions. Next, ditch the Protestant work ethic. Both traits run contrary to everything that PWT stand for. They are firm believers in introspection, and no one can introspect if he's trying to do things all the time. PWT believe in having a lot of reserve built up for when times get hard, so they spend a lot of time reserving. The benefits of achieving this uplifted state of mind are obvious when you consider the marked absence of stress-related disorders such as ulcers, tension headaches, and skin rashes among PWT.

There are a host of peripheral benefits that PWT also enjoy as a result of this philosophy. For instance, during the last two decades not a single PWT has died in an airplane collision, nor have any perished in a fire in a legitimate theater or in any restaurant with waiters. Though rumored to have frequent religious lapses, the average PWT is a disciplined observer of the Sabbath. Further, most PWT families will encourage individuals to have two or three other "special" days during the week to repose and introspect. Blue Mondays are a noted PWT phenomenon, and few realize that it was the PWT who first started TGIF observances throughout America. During all these periods, individuals go into deep reserve and can only be roused by a major family dispute or a shortage of beer.

PWT

WHY PWT?

America has always had a need for a lesser class citizen. For years we were able to thrive by importing various groups, but demand finally exceeded supply. Fortunately, the hearty and durable PWT were being refined in the South all the while. And now the time has come for them to take their rightful place below America's mainstream as the bedrock of our culture. Who else is going to staff our armies? Who else is going to buy all the late night TV products? Where will the future of bowling lead without PWT? And what about all those used cars and stereos? Do you want to junk the whole system? We *need* PWT.

Though it's done through an incredibly indirect system, PWT control the economy with their active third-ownership by keeping our commercial and industrial refuse employed productively. Just seeing a PWT family amid all the squalor makes the average person feel a lot better. Fortunately, there is an almost inexhaustible supply of PWT in the South. For years Yankees have come to the South strictly to experience the delight of PWT watching, but in the near future there will be enough PWT so that we'll be able to export enough even for the North. Until then, you will simply have to be in the South to observe quality PWT firsthand.

100% PO

WOVEN GA

PWT

Here in the Sunbelt, among the kudzu and Spanish moss, lurks perhaps the quintessential strain of Americans: Poor White Trash. They are the living refinement of our mighty nation's nearly four centuries of history, the ultimate genetic distillation of both physical and intellectual qualities. Products of a farsighted and intense inbreeding effort, PWTs are something else.

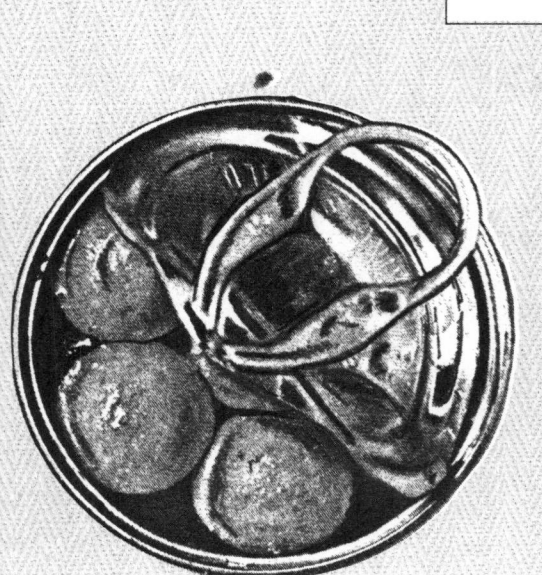

COONHOUNDS

If the transplanted Yankee decides to purchase a dog, he will definitely want to get a coonhound. It makes no difference whether or not you will ever hunt coons. Coonhounds are usually very mild mannered and make great house pets, hassocks, and doorstops. They actually run and are quite animated while hunting at night, but during the daylight hours they are extremely lethargic; their best trick is to play dead. The surest way to choose a coonhound is to judge it at rest, in the back of a pickup, where a championship hound will prove itself quickly. Simply take the dog and put it in the back of your truck. Drive around a little and observe it. If it gets excited and climbs all over the place, you should forget it; there's nothing worse than a hyperactive coonhound. If, on the other hand, the dog goes to sleep, you have a champion on your hands.

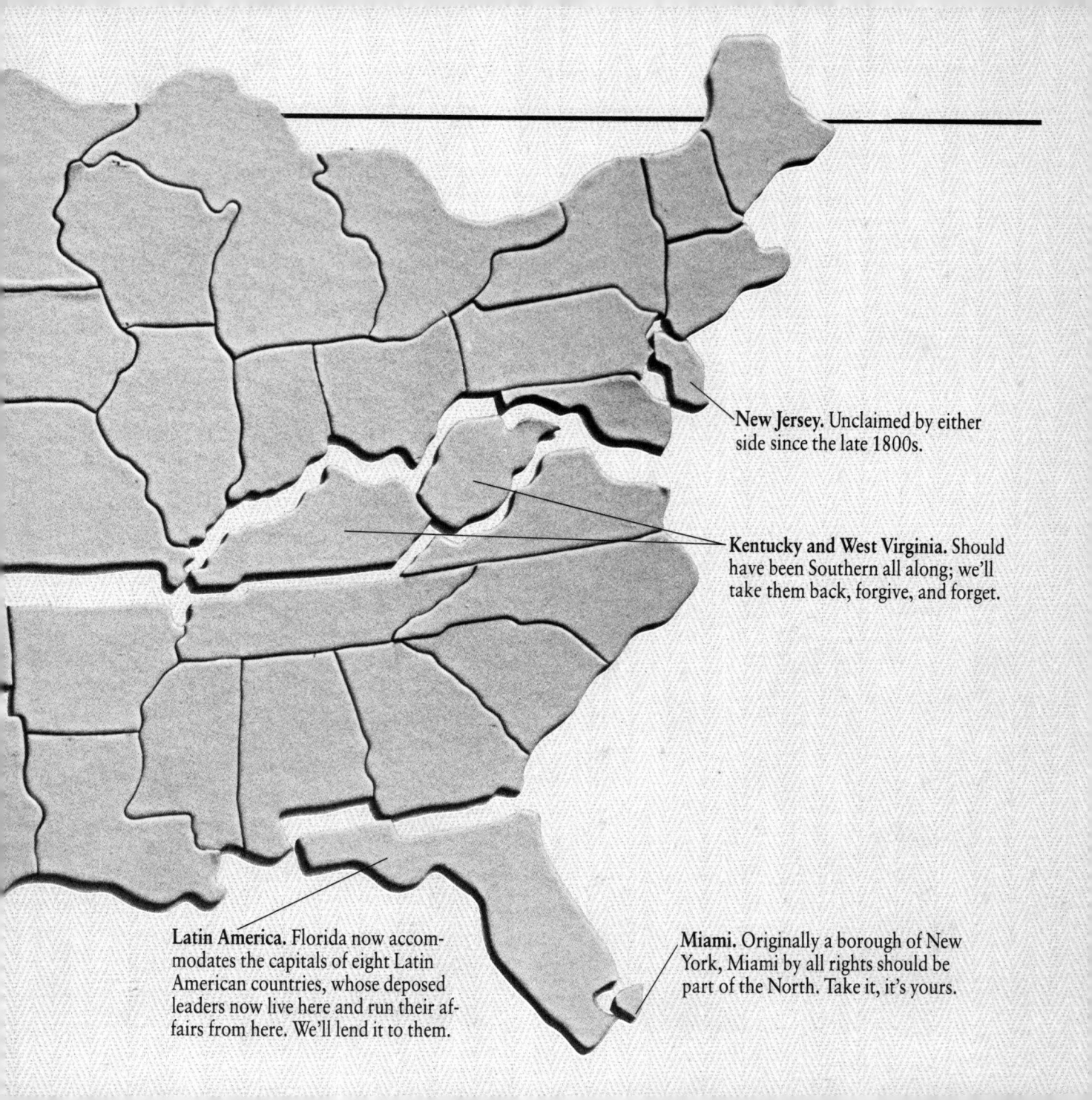

New Jersey. Unclaimed by either side since the late 1800s.

Kentucky and West Virginia. Should have been Southern all along; we'll take them back, forgive, and forget.

Latin America. Florida now accommodates the capitals of eight Latin American countries, whose deposed leaders now live here and run their affairs from here. We'll lend it to them.

Miami. Originally a borough of New York, Miami by all rights should be part of the North. Take it, it's yours.

THE MASON-DIXON LINE REVISITED

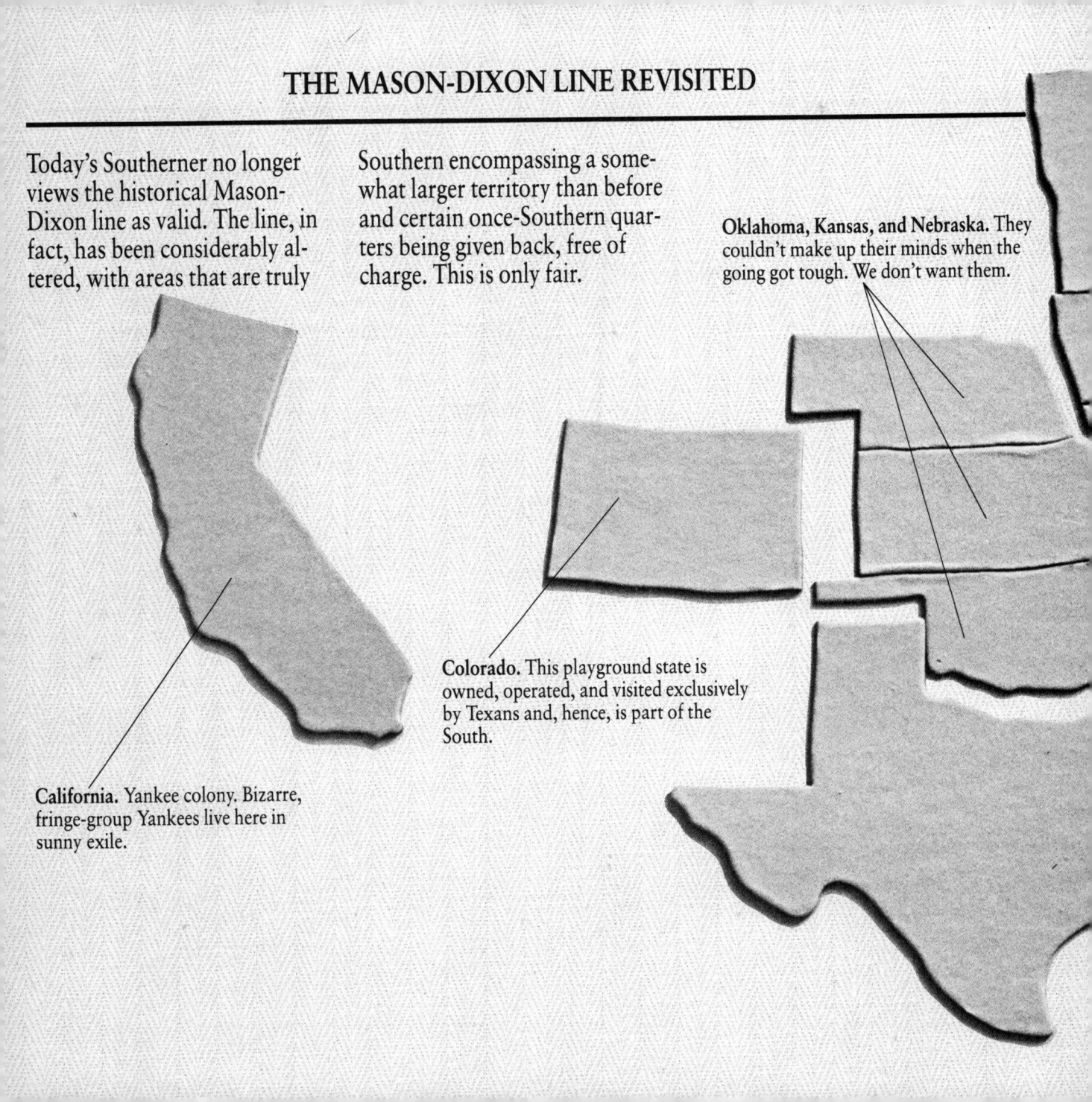

Today's Southerner no longer views the historical Mason-Dixon line as valid. The line, in fact, has been considerably altered, with areas that are truly Southern encompassing a somewhat larger territory than before and certain once-Southern quarters being given back, free of charge. This is only fair.

Oklahoma, Kansas, and Nebraska. They couldn't make up their minds when the going got tough. We don't want them.

Colorado. This playground state is owned, operated, and visited exclusively by Texans and, hence, is part of the South.

California. Yankee colony. Bizarre, fringe-group Yankees live here in sunny exile.

THE SOUTHERN PERSPECTIVE

Southerners live at a somewhat slower pace than most primates. Newcomers to the South often misinterpret our laconic conversational style and our general deliberativeness as signs of sloth, but this is not really accurate. The actual truth is that Southerners have learned to live life in a relaxed state of grace. Yankees who have not achieved this condition can often get by down here simply by throwing away their wrist watches and taking large doses of lithium.

It is extremely embarrassing for a Southerner to be discovered doing any real work, especially indoors (many perform their labors late at night and behind closely drawn curtains, lest anyone perceive them as unduly greedy or ambitious). Most have great faith in predestination and believe that if you work too much, you're fiddling with fate, or trying to stack the deck in your favor. That's cheating and that ain't godly, and it's sure to get you in trouble next time around. In fact, judgment can even come in this life: if you're a chronic workaholic and get caught in the act, they'll send you back to Cleveland.

THE SOUTH
MADE SIMPLER

By Michael Hicks

**Texas
Monthly**®
Press